Cambridge El‹

CW00538145

Elements in Internationa
edited by
Jon C. W. Pevehouse
University of Wisconsin-Madison
Tanja A. Börzel
Freie Universität Berlin
Edward D. Mansfield
University of Pennsylvania

SOCIAL MEDIA AND INTERNATIONAL RELATIONS

Sarah Kreps
Cornell University

CAMBRIDGE
UNIVERSITY PRESS

CAMBRIDGE
UNIVERSITY PRESS

University Printing House, Cambridge CB2 8BS, United Kingdom

One Liberty Plaza, 20th Floor, New York, NY 10006, USA

477 Williamstown Road, Port Melbourne, VIC 3207, Australia

314–321, 3rd Floor, Plot 3, Splendor Forum, Jasola District Centre,
New Delhi – 110025, India

79 Anson Road, #06–04/06, Singapore 079906

Cambridge University Press is part of the University of Cambridge.

It furthers the University's mission by disseminating knowledge in the pursuit of
education, learning, and research at the highest international levels of excellence.

www.cambridge.org
Information on this title: www.cambridge.org/9781108826815
DOI: 10.1017/9781108920377

First published 2020

A catalogue record for this publication is available from the British Library.

ISBN 978-1-108-82681-5 Paperback
ISSN 2515-706X (online)
ISSN 2515-7302 (print)

Social Media and International Relations

Elements in International Relations

DOI: 10.1017/9781108920377
First published online: July 2020

Sarah Kreps
Cornell University

Author for correspondence: Sarah Kreps, Sarah.kreps@gmail.com

Abstract: Democracies have long been credited with advantages ranging from sound governance to wartime effectiveness. Advantages accrue largely because the marketplace of ideas–freedom of expression, freedom of the press–enables a genuine debate about the virtues and vices of different policies in ways that inform the public, enable accountability, and produce better policy outcomes. This Element argues that the rise of social media undermines those democratic advantages. When citizens in the democratic populace turn to the marketplace of ideas, they increasingly confront misinformation, often strategically deployed by foreign actors seeking to exploit polarization in the political landscape and undermine trust in domestic institutions. Those actors can succeed because liberal democratic principles enshrine the media openness that becomes susceptible to foreign interference. Autocratic regimes have advantages because they can erect high barriers to entry into their own media markets. They can censor, counter, or even cut access to social media, which inoculates themselves from foreign influence and serves as a regime-preserving function. This Element updates these fundamental theories of international relations in light of changes to the media landscape and offers important insights into democratic governance and the conduct of conflict.

Keywords: mass media, public opinion, international relations, diplomacy

ISBNs: 9781108826815 (PB), 9781108920377 (OC)
ISSNs: 2515-706X (online), 2515–7302 (print)

Contents

1 Introduction

In 2018, legislators on Capitol Hill grilled Facebook Chief Executive Officer Mark Zuckerberg about the role of the social media platform in enabling foreign interference in the 2016 presidential election. Senator Orrin Hatch asked about Facebook's ability to generate revenue: "So, how do you sustain a business model in which users don't pay for your service?" he asked. Zuckerberg responded, "Senator, we run ads." To which Hatch responded, "I see. That's great."[1]

Except it was not all great and in fact the ads were one of the culprits in the 2016 presidential election. Russian interference in the election included buying Facebook ads that targeted and intended to inflame individuals on the basis of race, gender, and partisanship.[2] One ad consisted of a Confederate flag and verbiage saying "Heritage, not hate. The South will rise again!" Another was labeled "Blacktivist," indicating that the Black Panthers had been "dismantled by US government because they were black men and women standing up for justice and equality."[3] Facebook has since instituted new policies intended to constrain foreigners' ability to buy political ads. The mechanism involves a verification process that requires adjudicating the definition of a "political ad," which casts a wide net that has led to many false positives – groups inadvertently snared despite not being political in nature.[4] Measures to regulate the platform to make it safe for democracy may actually undermine it. In the same testimony, Senator Mark Warner (D-VA) asserted, "The era of the Wild West is coming to an end." He then said, "Where we go from here is an open question," signaling an awareness of the dilemma democracies face in a twenty-first-century information environment.[5]

This Element seeks to address some of those open questions. What are the features of social media that invite the prospect of foreign interference? More generally, what are the ways in which the nexus of information operations and the Internet can be deployed as tools of warfare? Are democracies more susceptible to online manipulation than nondemocracies? How do states assert digital sovereignty to provide access to their populace in ways that reflect

---

[1] Shannon Liao, "11 Weird and Awkward Moments from Two Days of Mark Zuckerberg's Congressional Hearing," *The Verge*, April 11, 2018.

[2] Samantha Bradshaw & Philip N. Howard, "Challenging Truth and Trust: A Global Inventory of Organized Social Media Manipulation." Working Paper 2018.1. Oxford, UK: Project on Computational Propaganda. comprop.oii.ox.ac.uk. 26 pp

[3] Scott Shane, "These Are the Ads Russia Bought on Facebook in 2016," *The New York Times*, November 1, 2017.

[4] Russell Brandom, "Facebook's New Political Ad Policy Is Already Sweeping Up Non-campaign Posts," *The Verge*, May 29, 2018.

[5] Warner Social Media Hearing, September 5, 2018, www.warner.senate.gov/public/index.cfm /2018/9/warner-social-media-hearing-opening-statement

national-level values? How are new technologies tapping into these democratic vulnerabilities? Lastly, what forms of governance might patch those vulnerabilities?

This Element answers those questions by examining social media as an actor in international relations. Zuckerberg has said, "in a lot of ways Facebook is more like a government than a traditional company."[6] This analysis takes that assertion seriously. Although the 2016 election highlighted the potential for foreign governments to employ social media for strategic advantages, the particular mechanisms of influence remain poorly understood. This research is the first to advance a theoretical framework of social media's influence on international relations, which I develop by incorporating insights from the "democratic dilemma."[7] As scholars of American politics have pointed out, democratic governance is characterized by a dilemma in that it depends on inputs from the populace, but on many issues, the populace is insufficiently informed to offer well-reasoned opinions.[8] In part because they are uninformed but also because most political issues are complicated and contested, the populace has a degree of ambivalence on most issues, which means they can have "opposing considerations on most issues, that is, considerations that might lead them to decide the issue either way."[9]

To resolve the knowledge deficits and ambivalence, individuals seek information from their media environment. Fundamental aspects of this democratic process are similar whether the media is new or old: the public pursues information to make good decisions. The marketplace of ideas has always trafficked in distortionary influences, including foreign actors using propaganda to try to influence public opinion. The phenomenon of foreign actors insinuating themselves into the media – and therefore political debates – is not new. Several factors distinguish social media from traditional media in terms of potential for manipulation.

First, because it is open access, anyone can post. Second, misinformation spreads faster and further than accurate information because it is often more clever, counterintuitive, or provocative.[10] Third, regulation is difficult. Social media sites and their fact-checking partners (e.g., Politifact or Snopes) can identify "fake news" and flag stories as "inaccurate," but efforts have also

---

[6] Franklin Foer, "Facebook's War on Free Will," *The Guardian*, September 19, 2017.

[7] Arthur Lupia and Mathew McCubbins, *The Democratic Dilemma: Can Citizens Learn What They Need to Know?* (Cambridge University Press, 1998).

[8] Ibid.

[9] John Zaller and Stanley Feldman, "The Political Culture of Ambivalence: Ideological Responses to the Welfare State," *American Journal of Political Science*, 36: 579–616; 585.

[10] Peter Dizikes, "Study: On Twitter, False News Travels Faster than True Stories," *MIT News*, March 8, 2018.

been plagued by accusations that they do so with an ideological eye, raising free-speech flags. Adding in artificial intelligence–generated stories scales up both the number and credibility of misinformation. What happens when millions of similar-but-not-identical stories hit people's feeds? There's no way for Facebook to flag or take down all of those stories in one fell swoop, as each one is unique. Put differently, Internet platforms have developed an ability to counteract propaganda at human scale. But they do not have the mechanisms to counteract it at machine-generated scale.

Emerging artificial intelligence (AI) tools significantly lower the barrier of entry to a widespread propaganda campaign. While the campaigns previously had to hire hundreds of staff to produce their content – a costly endeavor, especially for an operation that likely wants to remain under the radar – now most of that content generation can be automated away. In other words, almost anyone could theoretically run a disinformation campaign at the scale of Russia's just a few years ago – for a fraction of the price.

In this context, the open media environment of a democracy is particularly susceptible to foreign influence whereas the comparatively closed media environment of a nondemocracy provides efficient ways for these governments to censor, cut, or counter social media in ways that promote regime survival. Although social media platforms are increasingly aware of the role they play in altering the aperture of influence, the inherent features of these platforms – open, susceptible to misinformation, and imperfectly monitored – suggest that the political consequences, especially for democracies, are likely to remain. As the empirical evidence of this Element shows, misinformation does not necessarily succeed by changing minds but by sowing confusion, undermining trust in information and institutions, and eroding shared reference points that are the basis of coherent foreign policy.[11]

The focus on social media in international relations puts at least three major debates in its crosshairs. One has to do with the enduring strength of the state in international politics. In the 1970s, Keohane and Nye painted a scenario of a global village, in which the state's influence was secondary to multinational corporations, transnational social movements, and international organizations.[12] By the 1990s, they acknowledged that "the state has been more resilient" than they anticipated.[13] But technology raises questions about

---

[11] A 2019 interview between Twitter CEO Jack Dorsey and ReCode's Kara Swisher revealed Dorsey's awareness of corporate responsibility to make the platform safer, but the exchange also pointed to the technological challenges of doing so. See Rachel Kraus, "This Twitter Interview with CEO) Jack Proves the Platform Is Very Confusing," *Mashable*, February 12, 2019.

[12] Robert Keohane and Joseph Nye, *Power and Interdependence* (Pearson, 2011).

[13] Robert Keohane and Joseph Nye, "Power and Interdependence in the Information Age," *Foreign Affairs*, September/October 1998, 82.

whether those assertions were premature. Referring to the potential for social media to upend state sovereignty, Alec Ross, a technology adviser in the Obama Administration, spoke of Twitter as "the single most disruptive force for the sovereign state since the concept was founded with the 1648 Treaty of Westphalia. I don't think the Internet is going to take an eraser to state wars, but is inherently anti-state."[14] The reason is that large commercial monopolies have impacts well beyond state borders. The user experience is inherently transnational. They also have divisive impacts within states. The proliferation of fake news on social media polarizes societies and erodes trust in other citizens and institutions, thereby detracting from the country's ability to solve policy problems.[15]

This Element argues, however, that while the Internet was grounded in a sovereign-less architecture – hence the "world wide web" – states have gradually but surely asserted national law and sovereignty to control their constituents' use. China's "Great Firewall" is based on a principle of "internet sovereignty" in which "the internet is under the jurisdiction of Chinese sovereignty" and "laws and regulations clearly prohibit the spread of information that contains content subverting state power, undermining unity [or] infringing upon national honor or interests."[16] Iran, Russia, and North Korea have crafted their own country-specific access networks to minimize access to potential dissidents. The European Union created the General Data Protection Regulation (GDPR) that limits the transfer of personal data outside the European Union. All of these moves are reasserting, not disrupting, the Westphalian primacy of states.[17] One reason they can do that is that while the Internet and social media seem like software, they are ultimately grounded in hardware: fiberoptic cables, servers, and routers. Russia's "sovereign internet" law actually applies new hardware, a particular piece of hardware called the Deep Packet Inspection (DPI) technology provided by Russia's telecom agency that engages in censorship and surveillance.[18]

By suggesting that social media may be eroding democratic governance and conferring advantages to nondemocracies, this research also mediates a second major debate. Whether democracies are more effective in wartime has been a long-standing debate. So-called triumphalists suggests that in a democracy,

---

[14] Quoted in Patrikarakos, *War in 140 Characters.*: How Social Media is Reshaping Conflict in the Twenty-First Century (New York, NY: Basic Books, 2017).

[15] Lee Rainie and Andrew Perrin, "Key Findings about Americans' Declining Trust in Government and Each Other," *Pew*, July 22, 2019.

[16] Samuel Woodhams, "The Rise of Internet Sovereignty and the World Wide Web?" *The Globe Post*, April 23, 2019.

[17] Akash Kapur, "The Rising Threat of Digital Nationalism," *Wall Street Journal*, November 1, 2019.

[18] Mary Ilyushina, Nathan Lodge and Hadas Gold, "Russia Rolls Out Its 'Sovereign Internet': Is It Building a Digital Iron Curtain?" *CNN*, November 1, 2019.

a "relatively open marketplace of ideas engendered by a free press decreases the chances that democratic leaders will engage in foolhardy wars."[19] The perspective challenged a more skeptical view of democracy advanced by Walter Lippmann early in the previous century. In two separate accounts, Lippmann saw reality as perception rather than fixed,[20] which enabled leaders to craft and sell narratives through mass media. Pessimism about "the original dogma of democracy"[21] casts the public as pawns of political elites, a perspective that has found contemporary adherents, fueled by recent wars in which the media appeared complicit in the case for conflict rather than playing the devil's advocate role for which it has been theoretically ascribed.[22]

Social media has further muddled this debate. The information environment may be more democratic in an era of social media, insofar as anyone can generate content and moderation is limited, unconstrained by overarching editorial standards. It is also, however, less democratic because of its vulnerability to either inaccurate content or content provided by foreign governments or their proxies whose interests subvert the democratic process. Autocracies, in contrast, can neutralize the insidiousness of social media by censoring, controlling, or cutting off access altogether. Although censoring or cutting off access may be a signal of weakness, autocracies can nonetheless better control inflammatory content than democracies. The upshot is that Internet sovereignty may apply unevenly across regime types, and democracies may be at a comparative disadvantage in terms of vulnerability to outside interference relative to autocracies.

Lastly, the research speaks to a third major debate, the degree to which the Internet can be weaponized. In a 1995 book called *Information Warfare: Chaos on the Electronic Superhighway,* Winn Schwartau foreshadowed that "as the National Information Infrastructure grows and evolves into everyman's electronic superhighway, are we opening the doors to an electronic cold war?"[23] Just over two decades later, Russia was accused of influencing the United States presidential election through disinformation campaigns that originated with Russian groups tied to the Kremlin, were disseminated on the social media site Facebook, and rippled through numerous other online sites.

---

[19] Dan Reiter and Allan Stam, *Democracies at War* (Princeton University Press, 2002), 23.

[20] Walter Lippmann, *The Phantom Public* (New York: Harcourt Brace, 1925), 1933.

[21] Walter Lippmann, *Public Opinion* (Harcourt, Brace and Company, 1922), chapter XV.

[22] Chaim Kaufmann, "Threat Inflation and the Failure of the Marketplace of Ideas: The Selling of the Iraq War," *International Security*, 29, 1 (Summer 2004), 5–48; Jon Western, *Selling Intervention and War: The Presidency, the Media, and the American Public* (Johns Hopkins University Press, 2005).

[23] Winn Schwartau, *Information Warfare: Chaos on the Electronic Superhighway.* (Thunder's Mouth Press, 1994).

Although Russia has been accused of infiltrating election-related computer systems to discern weaknesses in the twenty states it targeted, the focus of scrutiny has been on the array of Internet-based activities that Russia conducted to influence attitudes in the United States, and in turn voter turnout, in the election. In particular, Russia is thought to have used both the official government intelligence agencies but also the Internet Research Agency (IRA), a Russian company engaged in online influence, to distribute either disinformation or socially divisive information on social media.[24] The goal was to influence attitudes about particular policies by way of undermining trust in democratic institutions and eroding American power abroad. It was also to shape attitudes about particular presidential candidates, which also would affect the bilateral relationship with Russia by trying to shift the balance of power to a more pro-Russian candidate. Both goals hinged on harvesting information about user behavior, which Russia allegedly obtained from a research group Cambridge Analytica. Then, based on psychologically profiling users based on their voting preferences, political views, and foreign policy, hyper-targeted particular demographics with provocative stories, memes, and political advertisements for which these groups would be most susceptible or receptive.[25] Facebook concluded that IRA content reached 140 million of its users.[26]

When former Director of the Federal Bureau of Investigation Robert Mueller testified to Congress about his investigation into Russia's interference in the 2016 elections, he spoke not just in the past tense but present and future: "They're doing it as we sit here," he said, continuing by saying that their interference will be "the new normal."[27] Until now, their ability to interfere has been limited by resources and bandwidth. Individuals who have worked at the Internet Research Agency, a Russian company that engages in online influence operations on behalf of Russian political interests, work twelve-hour shifts, writing articles or blog posts about topics that the government has assigned.[28] The demands are onerous because individuals must create new content, since searchable text would instantly reveal content that is plagiarized or recycled.

---

[24] www.justice.gov/file/1035477/download

[25] Danny Hakim and Matthew Rosenberg, "Data Firm Tied to Trump Campaign Talked Business with Russians," *The New York Times*, March 17, 2018.

[26] Alex Hern, "Facebook to Tell Users if They Interacted with Russia's 'Troll Army'" *The Guardian*, November 23, 2017.

[27] Julie Hirschfeld Davis and Mark Mazzetti, "Highlights of Robert Mueller's Testimony to Congress," *The New York Times*, July 24, 2019.

[28] Neil MacFarquhar, "Inside the Russian Toll Factory: Zombies and a Breakneck Pace," *The New York* Times, February 18, 2018; Adrian Chen, "The Agency," *The New York Times*, June 2, 2015.

Russia receives much of the attention having to do with online misinformation campaigns and foreign election interference, but the technology is accessible, affordable, and therefore diffusing quickly. New AI tools that can make the generation of large-scale synthetic text easy and more authentic stand to accelerate the diffusion even further. Already, seventy countries have engaged in Internet misinformation campaigns. Most of these are directed toward domestic audiences – for example, Ethiopia's government enlisted people to engage in online operations that aimed to bolster support for the ruling party. At least seven countries, however – in addition to Russia, China, India, Iran, Pakistan, Saudi Arabia, and Venezuela – have engaged in larger-scale misinformation campaigns across borders. Those are just the government-linked efforts.[29] In 2017, days before the French presidential election, Canadian and American-linked Twitter accounts spread 20,000 hacked emails from President Macron on an anonymous board 4chan, information that went viral with the aid of bots in the days before the election. National rules mandating media blackouts prevented an effective response from Macron, but the contents had spread widely online, a degree of electoral destabilization that Macron analogized to the 2016 American election in terms of undermining trust in electoral institutions and process.[30]

As the number and type of actor involved in these campaigns increases, the prospects of deterrence become even more complicated, almost futile. Indeed, while "cyber Pearl Harbor" scenarios – which would entail a cyberattack whose kinetic effects approximate a conventional attack – have tended to dominate policy debates,[31] the far more insidious type of online operation is the type of misinformation campaign that malicious actors can and will perpetrate via social media. The misuse of social media as a form of information operations is more mundane, legal, and an open secret that hides in plain sight. Foreign governments seem to have a role but one they do not acknowledge. Perhaps as a result, the public reports that it does not support aggressive forms of retaliation in response to foreign governments engaging in online misinformation campaigns.[32] Deterrence of these attacks, which would hinge on both some acknowledgement of the foreign actor and a credible commitment to use overwhelming force as retaliation for an attack, rests on shaky ground. The research

---

[29] Davey Alba and Adam Satariano, "At Least 70 Countries Have Had Disinformation Campaign, Study Finds," *The New York Times*, September 26, 2019.

[30] "Macron Says Hacked Documents Have Been Mixed with False Ones to 'Sow Doubt and Disinformation," *Agence France Presse*, January 12, 2018.

[31] See, inter alia, Adam Segal, The Hacked World Order: Hoow Nations Fight, Trade, Maneuver, and Manipulate in the Digital Age (Public Affairs, 2016), 86.

[32] Sarah Kreps and Jacquelyn Schneider, "Escalation Firebreaks in the Cyber, Conventional, and Nuclear Domains: Moving beyond Effects-Based Logics," Journal of Cyber Security, forthcoming; Michael Tomz and Jessica Weeks, "Public Opinion and Foreign Electoral Intervention," working paper.

therefore speaks to the dilemmas of deterrence in cyber more generally and malicious activity that "falls below the level of armed conflict"[33] in ways that undermine the credibility of an aggressive response.

To situate these debates, Section 2 outlines how the media theoretically functions in the democratic marketplace of ideas. It then introduces social media and points to the ways in which it differs qualitatively and qualitatively from traditional media. Section 3 develops the mechanisms through which social media could be used as a weapon of war, notably because of the offense-dominance of the platform and the psychology through which it affects individual decision-making. Section 4 then shows how these mechanisms may affect foreign policy heterogeneously depending on regime type. Democracies, with the relatively open information environment, are comparatively more vulnerable than nondemocracies, where leaders can cut, censor, or contest messages that might be threatening to regime stability.[34]

Next, in Section 5, this Element presents empirical evidence on public attitudes about social media and the erosion of trust in institutions. The central feature of the Section is an experiment that uses artificial intelligence (AI) to generate synthetic text, comparing it with human-written news stories to understand the public's ability to judge the credibility of online content. In October 2019, Zuckerberg said, "I generally believe that as a principle, people should decide what is credible, what they want to believe and who they want to vote for, and I don't think that that should be something that we want tech companies, or any kind of other company [to] do."[35] Evidence suggests that the public is not poised to judge what is credible, however, which raises questions of regulation more broadly. The evidence also suggests, however, that online misinformation does not necessarily change views about foreign policy issues such as North Korea and immigration, but it does muddy the marketplace of ideas. If individuals cannot tell fact from fiction, they come to believe nothing, perhaps other than information that confirms their partisan priors. Polarization intensifies, shared reference points disintegrate, and trust in institutions erodes, leaving foreign policy cohesion as the collateral damage.

The Element closes with a discussion about the ways social media companies have gestured toward governance and whether the cure, self-regulation, is worse than the disease, insufficient monitoring.

---

[33] US Department of Defense, "Department of Defense Cyber Strategy Summary," September 2018, https://media.defense.gov/2018/Sep/18/2002041658/-1/ 1/1/CYBER_STRATEGY_SUMMARY_FINAL.PDF.

[34] Democracies can also use information strategically and, in fact, passed legislation in 2012 "to authorize the domestic dissemination of information and material about the United States intended primarily for foreign audiences, and for other purposes" through the Smith-Mundt Modernization Act. Nonetheless, autocracies can still control their citizens' access to this information.

[35] "Facebook's Mark Zuckerberg: Private Companies Should Not Censor Politicians," *CNN*, October 18, 2019.

Although the Element focuses broadly on social media and international politics, many of the examples draw on the way Russia has used social media, largely because of the amount of investigatory work stemming from the 2016 American election. Further, the Mueller testimony suggests that Russia represents an ongoing and future player in online media manipulation. The Element, however, invoking the Prussian strategist Clausewitz, construes the topic of social media and international politics far more broadly as an example of war. It looks at episodes of how autocratic governments use social media to prosecute conflict against domestic groups, such as the Myanmar government inciting violence against minority groups via social media. It examines the way domestic political actors in both democracies such as the United States and the United Kingdom and nondemocracies such as China deploy social media in ways that paint their candidacy or regime in favorably to bolster domestic support.

It also speaks to potential shifts in China's strategic use of social media. In the Covid-19 pandemic, China increasingly looked more like it was taking a page from Russia's playbook, generating and distributing misinformation about the US response to the virus with an eye toward undermining trust in the government and polarizing the American electorate.[36] The goal is not just to offer a rendering of inept American leadership but to sing the praises of Chinese response or the generosity of China's supply of either personal protection equipment or merely time, taking the early brunt of the virus to let the rest of the world prepare accordingly.[37]

Actors have always used information in strategic ways. The difference now is the speed and scale. Social media quickly amplifies information – disproportionately disinformation – and AI-based tools scale up the production of misinformation to a point where it is indistinguishable from real information. Nondemocracies have a comparative advantage in this context by virtue of being able to control both the flow and content compared to democracies where efforts to flag misinformation both look politically motivated and, as the empirical analysis in this Element shows, are largely ineffective. In this context, the answer to technology may actually be *more* technology, since the same AI tools that create misinformation can be best at detecting it. But it may also be low-tech media literacy campaigns that help individuals identify the patterns of misinformation. Only then will the public will be poised to adjudicate credibility in ways that Zuckerberg deemed necessary for the proper functioning of media and democracy.

---

[36] Edward Wong, Matthew Rosenberg and Julian Barnes, "Chinese agents helped spread messages that sowed virus panic in US, Officials Say," *New York Times*, 23 April 2020.

[37] Laura Rosenberger, "China's coronavirus information operations," *Foreign Affairs*, 22 April 2020.

2 Social Media as a Social and Political Force

In 1969, three months after Neil Armstrong took steps on the moon, another "first" took place, albeit with less ceremony. A graduate student from UCLA tried to send the first email, typing "L" and "O" to a computer at the Stanford Research Institute, not finishing the word "login" before the system crashed. The project was part of the military's Advanced Research Projects Agency whose mission was in fact indirectly connected to the moon landing. In 1958, the US government launched ARPA to deflect the potential for more Sputnik moments in which the Soviets outpaced the United States in technology. ARPA had set up primitive routers on the West Coast of the United States, connected to computers by telephone lines. The first email wasn't officially sent until 1971, when ARPANET connected fifteen computers.

Soon after, computer nodes in Norway and the United Kingdom were added to the project. Without some common "language," however, these computers could not talk to each other. Designers responded with "internetting" or "open-architecture networking." As long as computers adopted Transfer Control Protocol/Internet Protocol (TCP/IP), they could join the network. ARPANET then divided into the primarily civilian network and MILNET, the military operational network that was protected by encryption and restricted access control. ARPANET became the foundation for the contemporary Internet, an open network architecture whose contents were relatively unregulated.

In the earliest days of the Internet, the institutions and individuals all knew each other. As John Naughton observes, the early Internet

> was essentially a geek preserve, with a social ethos that was communal, libertarian, collaborative, occasionally raucous, anti-establishment and rich in debate and discussion. It had no commerce, no hierarchies … it was populated by people who either knew one another, or at least knew others' institutional affiliations. In that sense, cyberspace and the so-called real world existed as parallel universes.[38]

Many of these features define the current Internet, in particular, the openness, flat hierarchy, and more-than-occasional raucousness. Most different today is the magnitude of the Internet and anonymity. Today it is enormous and relatively anonymous even as social networks have brought individuals together. This Section explains social media, the scale, how it works, and its role in providing news before taking a step back into the ways it contrasts with traditional media. If social media were only a difference in degree from traditional media, then we would not need new theories or explanations for how individuals consume it in the process of familiarizing themselves with public

---

[38] John Naughton, "The Evolution of the Internet: From Military Experiment to General Purpose Technology," *Journal of Cyber Policy*, 1, 1 (2016), 5–28.

policies. I argue, however, that it is a difference in kind, such that we do need new ways of thinking about the way individuals consume media and how that affects foreign policy.

The Rise of Social Media

Building on the networked, collaborative features of the early Internet, a few kids in a college dorm decided they would leverage this architecture to share ideas about their peers. The platform became Facebook, which launched for Harvard undergrads in February 2004, then opened to other campuses in the Boston area, Ivy League, and universities in the United States and Canada, and then opened to the public in September 2006. It reached 50 million users within two years. By 2018, Facebook had 2.271 billion monthly users globally, followed by YouTube, with 1.8 billion.[39] To put the growth of users in perspective, initial social media sites such as MySpace had 75.9 million unique visitors per month at its 2008 peak. Facebook remains dominant globally, with 270 million users in India, 240 million in the United States, 85 million in Mexico, and 130 million in Brazil. In some developing countries, Facebook *is* the Internet because it is exempted from data plans and therefore offers a way to connect without cost.[40] Facebook has developed Free Basics, limited but free Internet service in about 65 countries including Mexico, Kenya, Pakistan, and the Philippines, that allows individuals to access about 150 sites and services. Critics have questioned the neutrality of the service, which essentially tiers access in ways that privilege certain sites and therefore content, but the result is that Free Basics has increased overall access to both Facebook and the Internet and consolidated Facebook's global dominance in the world of social media.[41]

One feature that distinguishes current social media from early versions is the degree to which individuals access these sites for news. As figure 1 shows, in 2018, 68% of American adults obtained their news from social media, compared to 49% of adults in 2012.[42] While more people still receive their news from television, the gap between online sources and television has narrowed to 7 points, and people obtain their news from online sources at twice the rate as print newspapers.[43] Social media platforms such as Reddit draw a larger

---

[39] David Cohen, "Facebook Reported 2.217 Billion Monthly Users, 1.495 Billion Daily Users at the End of Q3," *Ad Week*, October 31, 2018; Adi Robertson, "YouTube Has 1.8 Billion Logged-In Viewers Each Month," *The Verge*, May 3, 2018.

[40] www.mmtimes.com/business/technology/20685-facebook-free-basics-lands-in-myanmar.html

[41] Olivia Solon, "'It's Digital Colonialism': How Facebook's Free Internet Service Has Failed Its Users," *The Guardian*, July 22, 2017.

[42] www.journalism.org/2016/05/26/news-use-across-social-media-platforms-2016/; www.journalism.org/2018/09/10/news-use-across-social-media-platforms-2018/

[43] "Key Trends in Social and Digital News Media," *Pew*, October 4, 2017.

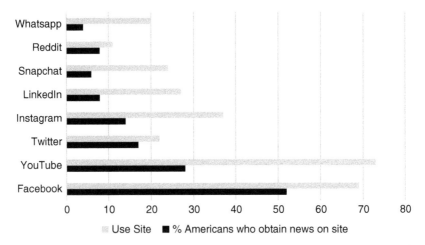

Figure 1 News use across social media networks in 2018. Source: Pew Research.

percentage of users to news (73%) compared to Facebook (68%). Facebook has the largest reach, however, because of the sheer number of people who use the site. Only 4% of Americans use Reddit compared to 68% of Americans who are on Facebook. Taken together, 43% of all Americans obtain their news from Facebook, compared to 21% for YouTube, the largest growing platform, up from 10% of people who obtained their news from YouTube in 2016.[44]

That the news environment has transformed is not evidence in and of itself of political consequences. Identifying the potential for political consequences first requires considering the ways in which differences between social and traditional media might open the door to a new set of changes in political participation, "activity that . . . has the intent or effect of influencing what the government does," which can include going to the polls, which affects the individuals who are elected and ultimately formulate foreign policy as well as expression of public attitudes, a public mood that percolates up into the sustainability of public policy.[45] To draw these contrasts, however, first requires taking a step back and outlining media theory, in particular the role of the media in foreign policy formation.

The Media as the Fourth Estate

Edmund Burke referred to the media as the "fourth Estate more important" than the other branches of democratic government. The expression refers to the separation of powers in which the legislature, executive, and judiciary represent

---

[44] www.journalism.org/2019/10/02/americans-are-wary-of-the-role-social-media-sites-play-in-delivering-the-news/; www.journalism.org/2018/09/10/news-use-across-social-media-platforms-2018/

[45] Sidney Verba, Kay Lehman Schlozman, and Henry Brady, *Voice and Equality: Civic Voluntarism in American Politics* (Harvard University Press, 1995).

the three main estates and the media acts as the additional and important check in the political system. In principle, it fulfills this role by providing a platform for competing views, presenting the concerns of aggrieved actors in the political landscape, or communicating developments in legislation.[46] It both provides politically relevant information and, by facilitating exchanges in the market-place of ideas, can also provide checks and balances against foolhardy policy proposals, including those related to war and peace.[47]

The traditional vehicles for politically relevant information – and the way through which media could exert political influence by informing the populace and in turn having a constraining effect on democratic governance – have been newspapers, radio, and television.[48] Their primary mechanism of influence involves reaching the domestic public, which then formulates opinions that have a bottom-up effect on decision-makers, who are elected by the public and therefore have incentives to hew closely to the public's preferences on issues of foreign policy.[49]

Traditional sources of media have undergone a number of transformations in recent years. In 2003, Matt Baum described changes in mass media coverage as a turn to "soft news," which meant news entertainment on television or radio, embodied by shows such as *Entertainment Tonight*, *The Daily Show*, or late-night comedians whose monologues touched on politics.[50] According to Baum, the burgeoning influence of soft news challenged the long-held conventional wisdom that the public would be uninformed about politics, including foreign policy. Rather, "changes in mass media coverage of foreign policy are almost certain to affect how at least some segments of the public understand and evaluate the political world ... in effect, democratizing access to information."[51]

The net foreign policy influence of those changes to media, however, is unclear. In a study of how the media writ large affects foreign policy, Baum and Potter depicted a number of theoretical ways that media could have foreign policy consequences. Decision makers influence media coverage through the decisions they make and events on the ground, the public affects the media because of market-driven considerations about public interests, the media affects public

---

[46] Julianne Schultz, *Reviving the Fourth Estate: Democracy, Accountability, and the Media* (Cambridge University Press, 2009), 1–4.

[47] Reiter and Stam, Democracies at War (Princeton University Press, 2002), 23.

[48] Matthew Baum and Philip B. K. Potter, *War and Democratic Constraint: How the Public Influences Foreign Policy* (Princeton University Press, 2015), 5.

[49] Matthew Baum and Philip B. K. Potter, "The Relationships between Mass Media, Public Opinion, and Foreign Policy: Toward a Theoretical Synthesis," *Annual Review of Political Science*, 11 (2008), 39–65; 41.

[50] Matthew Baum, *Soft News Goes to War: Public Opinion and American Foreign Policy in the New Media Age.* (Princeton University Press, 2003), ix.

[51] Ibid., 4.

opinion formation in terms of how they examine foreign policy proposals, and ultimately in a democracy, public preferences inform the political palatability of leaders' policy proposals. Yet as the authors concluded, "this web of causal arrows has become so dense that further investigation into these narrow individual pathways is likely to produce diminishing returns" (Figure 2).[52]

Further complicating the picture are those who fundamentally cast doubt on the strength of any of these causal arrows. Critiques take the form of those who question the independence of the mass media, suggesting that instead of objectively ferreting out dubious foreign policies, the media merely magnifies the top-down messages trotted out by political elites.[53] The media then is not an independent Fourth Estate that checks the other branches of government, especially the executive branch, but rather its mouthpiece.

Even further clouding the debate about the role of the media in the marketplace of ideas is that the Internet has changed how the public consumes news. The fundamental change consists of an increased public consumption of social media sites, defined as "web-based services that allow individuals to (1) construct a public or semi-public profile within a bounded system, (2) articulate

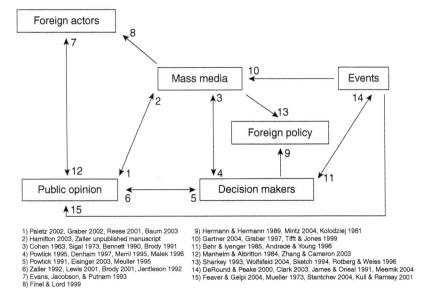

1) Paletz 2002, Graber 2002, Reese 2001, Baum 2003
2) Hamilton 2003, Zaller unpublished manuscript
3) Cohen 1963, Sigal 1973, Bennett 1990, Brody 1991
4) Powlick 1995, Denham 1997, Merril 1995, Malek 1996
5) Powlick 1991, Eisinger 2003, Meuller 1995
6) Zaller 1992, Lewis 2001, Brody 2001, Jentleson 1992
7) Evans, Jacobson, & Putnam 1993
8) Finel & Lord 1999

9) Hermann & Hermann 1989, Mintz 2004, Kolodziej 1981
10) Gartner 2004, Graber 1997, Tifft & Jones 1999
11) Behr & Iyengar 1985, Andrade & Young 1996
12) Manhelm & Albritton 1984, Zhang & Cameron 2003
13) Sharkey 1993, Wolfsfeld 2004, Sketch 1994, Rotberg & Weiss 1996
14) DeRound & Peake 2000, Clark 2003, James & Oneal 1991, Meemik 2004
15) Feaver & Gelpi 2004, Mueller 1973, Stantchev 2004, Kull & Ramsay 2001

Figure 2 "Web of causal arrows" linking media, the public, and decision makers. Baum and Potter, 2008.

[52] Matthew Baum and Philip B. K. Potter, "Mass Media, Public Opinion, and Foreign Policy: Toward a Theoretical Synthesis," *Annual Review of Political Science*, 11 (2008), 39–65; 41.
[53] Chaim Kaufman, "Threat Inflation".

a list of other users with whom they share a connection, and (3) view and traverse their list of connections and those made by others within the system."[54] These media sites have burgeoned both as focal points of social exchange and an important source of political news. Observing the rise of social media, Baum and Potter noted that "the information environment has fundamentally shifted over the past two decades, but scholarship has failed to keep pace."[55] Or as one journalist concluded, "no one can quite wrap their heads around what this thing [social media] has become."[56] The next section evaluates social media as a vehicle for political exchange and explains why it is more powerful tool of influence than traditional media.

Is Social Media Just Old Wine in New Media Bottles?

One view of social media is that it has clear antecedents to the Romans – that the Roman Colosseum was the YouTube of its time, for example – and that contemporary social ordering principles grounded in the Internet are nothing new.[57] This type of argument is meant to inoculate against perspectives that assign high degrees of causal weight to the flow of information online. If indeed social media finds close antecedents, whether in the Ancients or more recently in traditional media, then we do not need new theories that speak to the potential foreign policy consequences. Yet I argue that the differences in both degree and kind are significant. We cannot simply import existing theories – perhaps simply accelerating the causal effect of media on foreign policy – but rather need new accounts of how the consumption of new media, in particular social media, affects political behavior.

One major difference between traditional and social media is the open access of social media, meaning any individual can contribute, curate, and disseminate information. The Internet itself lacks central management and is meant to distribute information without privilege, preference, or bias on the basis of content or sender. The social media experience incorporates these principles. Individuals create content, the platform connects users with large numbers of people, users post without permission, and other users are privy to content.[58] As

---

[54] Danah Boyd and Nicole Ellison, "Social Network Sites: Definition, History, and Scholarship," *Journal of Computer-Mediated Communication*, 13, 1 (October 2007), 210–230.

[55] Matthew Baum and Philip B. K. Potter, "Media, Public Opinion, and Foreign Policy in the Age of Trump," *Journal of Politics*, 81, 2 (2019), 747–756.

[56] Alexis C. Madrigal "What Facebook Did to American Democracy," www.theatlantic.com/technology/archive/2017/10/what-facebook-did/542502/

[57] Jonathan Salem Baskin, *Histories of Social Media* (Society for New Communications Research, 2011).

[58] David Weinberger, "The Internet that Was (and Still Could Be), *The Atlantic* June 22, 2015, https://www.theatlantic.com/technology/archive/2015/06/medium-is-the-message-paradise-paved-internet-architecture/396227/

Chesney and Citron suggest, "thanks to smartphones, which make it easy to capture audio and video content, and social media platforms, which allow that content to be shared and consumed, people today can rely on their own eyes and ears to an unprecedented degree."[59] Individuals can become citizen journalists, collecting news and then posting original content they collect onto social media, which helps disseminate the information.

The democratization of media has its virtues in that it can provide a voice to the otherwise unempowered and sidestep the constraints of traditional media's editorial process. If traditional media skeptics are correct, then those editorial standards are an artificial straitjacket that can reinforce rather than challenge the groupthink of political elites.[60] A more optimistic read of editorial standards, however, is that on average, traditional media has a longer shadow of the future that includes a need to preserve the outlet's enduring credibility. The mantra is to "filter, then publish," editing, prioritizing, and rejecting before exposure to the public. In the social media world, the order is reversed: "publish, then filter."[61] Because the costs of posting content are low, as is the need for long-term credibility, individuals can post and allow mass audiences to sort after publication. The line between amateur and expert nearly disappears.[62]

A second difference between social and traditional media is the directionality of the information flow. Traditional media is unidirectional, in which the news-paper, for example, pushes information out to consumers who do not in turn dialogue with the original source. Social media, by contrast, produces a bi- or multi-directional flow of information that allows for messages to be amplified widely. By virtue of being networked, individuals are connected with friends, family, those individuals' networks, and beyond. Social media then stands to act as an enormous amplifier of content, providing instantaneous and global reach. The implications are that the flows of information are capable of "creating temporary portals or 'contact zones' between geographically dispersed cultures"[63] in ways that are impossible through traditional media sources.

Third, the behavioral psychology of the online experience and particular types of content can generate a degree of amplification that is muted in traditional media. Although the principle that "if it bleeds, it leads" – where fear-based

---

[59] Robert Chesney and Danielle Citron, "Deepfakes and the New Disinformation War," *Foreign Affairs*, Jan/Feb 2019.

[60] Kaufmann, "Threat Inflation".

[61] Clay Shirky, *Here Comes Everybody: The Power or Organizing without Organizations* (Penguin Books, 2009), 81.

[62] Andrew Keen, "The Cult of the Amateur," in Magnus Ramage (ed.), *Online Communication and Collaboration* (Routledge, 2010), pp. 251–256; 251.

[63] Henry Jenkins, "Pop Cosmopolitanism," in Globalization: Culture and Education in the New Millennium, 114.

stories crowd out blander content – applies to television and traditional print media, it intersects with the amplification dynamic of social media because of features peculiar to the Internet.[64] As Facebook realized early on, whereas the initial purpose of social media was to bring undergraduate students together, the scaled-up business model required growth, which meant luring people online, convincing them to stay, and cajoling their friends to do the same. The company grounded their growth strategy on behavioral psychology, leveraging the idea of "nudges" that frame choices in ways that nearly preordain outcomes by implicitly ranking the relative attractiveness of different options. [65] Organ donor buttons, they determined, would be a form of virtue signaling for friends, who would receive notifications, which were associated with dopamine hits that would generate more interest in and time on the social network. On the first day of the organ donor button's presence on Facebook, nationwide organ donor enrollment increased twentyfold,[66] revealing the scale and prospects for how other actors might manipulate social media for more nefarious ends. As one early Facebook engineer confessed, "if your job is to get that number up, at some point you run out of good, purely positive ways. You start thinking about 'Well, what are the dark patterns that I can use to get people to log back in?'"[67]

Generators of content realized that negative messages or fear could stimulate acute interest in the form of prolonged time on the website or shares with one's network. Indeed, the flip side of virtue signaling of a dopamine-inducing hit – and the invitation for manipulation by unsavory actors – is the vitriol-as-viral problem. Research on "viral content" – articles that generate thousands or millions of clicks – shows that positive-feeling content is one vehicle for going viral, but so is content that incites fear and distress. Studies on the correlates of clicks show that a combination of three characteristics piques online interest: valence, which is the positivity or negativity, with joy being a typical positive valence and fear being negative; arousal, ranging from excitement to relaxation, with anger being a high-arousal emotion; and dominance, ranging from submission to feeling in control, with admiration – viewed as a feeling that individuals have agency over – as high dominance.[68]

---

[64] Deborah Serany, "If It Bleeds, It Leads: Understanding Gear-Based Media," *Psychology Today*, June 7, 2011.

[65] Richard Thaler and Cass Sunstein, *Nudge: Improving Decisions about Health, Wealth, and Happiness* (Yale University Press, 2008).

[66] Evan Osnos, "Can Mark Zuckerberg Fix Facebook Before It Breaks Democracy?" *New Yorker*, September 17, 2018.

[67] Ibid.

[68] Kerry Jones, Kelsey Libert, and Kristin Tynski, "The Emotional Combinations That Make Stories Go Viral," *Harvard Business Review*, May 23, 2016.

Table 1 shows the most common combinations of how arousal and dominance combine to produce either negatively or positively valenced content as well as media examples of viral content that illustrates those categories. Overall, surprising, complicated, or extremely positive content is more likely to go viral. Only certain configurations of valence and dominance produce those feelings, however. As Table 1 suggests, emotions such as surprise, fear, and distress drive traffic. In terms of the prospect for the manipulation of social media, "the role of valence appears to be consistent among all indices of virality in both datasets, with negative valence contributing to higher virality."[69] Viral content can originate from actual events such as the cheetah jumping into a safari jeep. As of November 2019, at least four YouTube videos of cheetahs jumping into a safari jeep have garnered more than 1 million views.[70]

Users have also discovered, however, the virtues of inauthentic content for driving the type of emotional reaction associated with clicks, which is that this information spreads quickly. The term "fake news" has attracted considerable attention because of Donald Trump's prevalent use of the word, as well as the Western electoral cycles around 2016 that saw a spike in dubious online information. Here it refers to the basket of news that is "intentionally and

Table 1 *Most common* combinations of emotional attributes in viral articles. Adapted from Jones et al., 2016[71]

Arousal	Dominance	Valence	Media Example
High +	High	Positive or positive surprised (admiration, happiness, love)	Paramedics doing dishes after woman taken to hospital
High +	Low	Surprise mixed with only positive or surprise mixed with + (happiness and admiration) or – (fear, distress)	Cheetah jumps into jeep during safari
Low +	Low	Negative surprise (pity) or positive surprise	Cringe-worthy episode in sports

---

[69] Marco Guerini and Jacopo Staiano, "Deep Feelings: A Massive Cross-Lingual Study on the Relation between Emotions and Virality,"
[70] www.youtube.com/watch?v=auWdkqvvaw0
[71] Jones et al., "The Emotional Combinations."

verifiably false, and could mislead readers."[72] It can include misinformation, which is false information distributed without harmful intent, or disinformation, false information created and shared with harmful intent.

The problem with fake news is that, as Jonathan Swift wrote, "Falsehood flies, and the Truth comes limping after it." Facebook's top 100 fake news stories in 2019 were viewed over 158 million times, "enough to reach every registered voter at least once" as one study concluded, and twice the number of people who clicked on the Republican and Democratic Party Facebook pages. Far fewer see retractions, if any are issued – indeed, of those 100 stories, all of them remain on Facebook, including stories about Democratic members of Congress holding secret fundraisers with Islamic terror groups, another Democratic member of Congress proposing a motorcycle ban, and President Trump trying to impeach his vice president.[73]

High school students in Macedonia learned the virtues of fake news-based virality when they began posting fabricated stories on Facebook about American politics. In one case, a teenager posted a story from a campaign rally in which candidate Donald Trump slapped a member in the audience who had disagreed with him. The individual had located the story online, incorporated some of the text, posted and linked onto Facebook, and found that the article was shared hundreds of times, which led to ad revenue and incentives to continue posting more disingenuous stories.[74] The incentives of those generating content, whether individuals or state-run internet agencies, are therefore to be as polemical as possible, even if that information is either inaccurate or even wholly manufactured. Studies of humans' ability to discern accurate from false information show that individuals can identify false information such as hoaxes or fake news with accuracies between 53 percent and 78 percent, but that they are especially deceived when information is well referenced or they receive it multiple times, are politically biased, or have less education, in which case disinformation is more likely to have a strong impact.[75]

To be sure, traditional media has similar incentives of concern themselves with erosions of trust that come from inaccurate stories on their sites, but

---

[72] Edson Tandoc Jr., Zheng Wei Lim, and Richard Ling, "Defining 'Fake News': A Typology of Scholarly Definitions,"*Digital Journalism*, 6, 2 (2018), 137–153; 128.

[73] Ben Gilbert, "The 10 Most-Viewed Fake-News Stories on Facebook Were Just Revealed in a New Report," *Business Insider*, November 6, 2019; Dan Gilbert, "2020 Voters are Already Being Inundated by Fake News on Facebook," *Vice News*, November 6, 2019.

[74] Samanth Subramanian, "Inside the Macedonian Fake-News Complex," *Wired*, February 15, 2017.

[75] Srijan Kumar and Neil Shah, "False Information on Web and Social Media: A Survey," *arXiv* (2018), 1–35; 2.

platforms' efforts to moderate and filter those stories are imperfect at best, and damaging at worst when they are seen as ideologically biased.[76] Traditional media outlets typically have more aggressive gate-keeping strategies, whether through hiring trusted journalists in the first place or engaging in editing and fact-checking.

Fourth, algorithms built into social media are themselves susceptible to artificial efforts at amplification that would be impossible in a traditional media setting. Malicious actors have found a number of ways to amplify their message. Sock puppets allow users to circumvent bans or suspended sites or identities, masquerading as a legitimate, valid identity, the equivalent of an online pseudonym. Ultimately, the goal is to manipulate public opinion and garner support for an individual or organization online by creating an aura of support around that entity. Actors intending to manipulate viewers for nefarious ends can also engage in astroturfing, the use of a pseudonym to manufacture the perception of mass support to create a bandwagon effect in favor of a particular perspective.[77] To even further augment the reach, a number of governments have also relied on bots, which are used to mimic individual users but can be used en masse to overwhelm social media in ways that create an impression of a popular movement. Social media bots, estimated to be about 9–15 percent of active Twitter accounts, can manipulate the direction and sense of enthusiasm surrounding a political discussion and thereby affect the tenor of the overall debate.[78]Social media platforms are increasingly attuned to the practice and have tried to remove those accounts, giving rise to "cyborgs" (cyber organism) meant to appear more human but that leverage the amplification properties of a bot in ways that would reduce the prospects for detection.[79]

In short, social media appears to be both a difference in degree and in kind from traditional media. Its ability to amplify information reduces the time-space continuum, what Giddens referred to as "distanciation" or the ways in which time or space materially separates social interactions.[80] In this case, social

---

[76] Matthew Ingram, "Most Americans Say They Have Lost Trust in the Media," *Columbia Journalism Review*, September 12, 2018.

[77] Adam Bienkov, "Astroturfing: What Is It and Why Does It Matter?" *The Guardian*, February 8, 2012; Andrey Soshnikov, "Facebook Uncovers 'Russian-Funded' Misinformation Campaign," *BBC*, September 7, 2017.

[78] Onur Varol, Emilio Ferrara, Clayton Davis, Filippo Menczer, and Alessandro Flammini, "Online Human–Bot Interactions: Detection, Estimation, and Characterization," Proceedings of the Eleventh International AAAI Conference, 280–289; 280.

[79] Samantha Bradshaw and Philip Howard, "Troops, Trolls and Troublemakers: A Global Inventory of Organized Social Media Manipulation," *Propaganda Research Project*, working paper no. 2017.12, 11–12.

[80] Anthony Giddens: Critical Assessments, Volume 3 (Taylor and Francis, 1997), 28.

media can move information globally and instantaneously, compressing the time-space continuum insofar as it minimizes the separation between people and information. Section 3 moves from the theoretical differences between social and traditional media to the ways that actors can exploit the features of social media to achieve political aims.

3 Social Media as a Weapon of War

The Prussian strategist Clausewitz famously observed that war is a continuation of politics by other means. Less familiar to nonspecialists is Clausewitz's trinity of war, which elaborates on what he meant by war as a continuation of politics. He identified reason (the government), emotion and passion (the people), and chance (the military). Public opinion influences policy – in particular, the sustainability of a government's policy – just as it also influences military strategy, for example, through the public's tolerance of costs.

The trinity illustrates why war has included psychological operations, defined as:

> operations to convey selected information and indicators to foreign audiences to influence their emotions, motives, objective reasoning, and ultimately the behavior of foreign governments, organizations, groups, and individuals. The purpose of psychological operations is to induce or reinforce foreign attitudes and behavior favorable to the originator's objectives.[81]

The premise is that war is a political act and co-opting public opinion through the strategic deployment of information can favorably tilt the balance of support. This Section outlines the enduring interest of international actors in using information to generate support for their own political cause and undermine that for an adversary's. It then goes beyond the last Section's discussion of how social media differs from traditional media to suggest why it is well-suited to the particular goals of propaganda. It does so by advancing a theory of social media consumption before outlining the types of malicious actors that could exploit features of social media, specifically the openness, ability to amplify, and challenges to effective content moderation.

International Actors' Enduring Interest in Information Operations

Early antecedents of psychological warfare preview the way through which information operates as a tool of warfare. The Trojan horse, mythologized in Homer's writing of the *Iliad* in the eight century BC and about a period of

---

[81] https://fas.org/blogs/secrecy/2010/01/psyop/

imagined history in the thirteenth century BC, foreshadowed the writing of Greek philosophers such as Aristotle who believed that "the purpose of persuasion was to communicate a point of view and that knowledge and wisdom could only be secured through logic and reason."[82] Although Aristotle stipulated that reliance on facts would be most effective, the success of the Trojan horse pointed to more disingenuous paths to victory that later rulers embraced. Leaders in the Assyrian empire, for example, would draft documents that disingenuously reflected divine support in ways that were intended to shore up public support. Palaces were repositories of propaganda, through statues, inscriptions, and art, but rulers also crafted warnings for their subjects. One Assyrian king killed the soldiers who had attempted revolt, arraying their skins on pillars at the city gate to deter future revolts. As one account suggests, "it was a policy of terror coupled with one of propaganda, designed to keep conquered peoples down and to frighten potential enemies with graphic propagandist imagery and brutal psychology."[83]

Wartime elicited the deployment of information intended less to frighten enemies and more to convince their populations to acquiesce, or in the case of allies such as the United States, to end neutrality.[84] Winston Churchill famously described wartime propaganda as intrinsic and invaluable to war: "In wartime, truth is so precious that she should always be attended by a bodyguard of lies."[85] British broadcasting operated both as a source of inspiration to the domestic audience but also aimed to galvanize resistance in occupied Europe. Germany's propaganda chief Goebbels observed in 1944, "there is one way in which the British, despite the narrowness of their political thinking, are ahead of us – they know that news can be a weapon and are experts in its strategy."[86] He also asserted, "repeat a lie often enough and it becomes the truth," speaking to the "illusion of truth" attendant to information exposure, which is that with enough exposure to misinformation, people might believe its truth. Reality, accordingly, becomes malleable, which means that the sheer volume of exposure, even to information of dubious quality, can combine to convince the individual of a falsehood. Indeed, one study of exposure to fake news showed that other than for entirely implausible

---

[82] Philip Taylor, *Munitions of the Mind: A History of Propaganda from the Ancient World to the Present Era* (Manchester University Press, 2003), 15.

[83] Ibid., 24.

[84] Nicholas John Cull, *Selling War: The British Propaganda Campaign against American "neutrality" in World War II* (Oxford University Press, 1996).

[85] Remarks as delivered by General Fogleman, "Information Operations: The Fifth Dimension of Warfare," April 25, 1995, www.iwar.org.uk/iwar/resources/5th-dimension/iw.htm

[86] David Boyle, "Why the Taboo Tale of the BBC's Wartime Propaganda Battle Must Be Told," *The Guardian*, January 11, 2018.

statements – "the earth is a perfect square" – repetition of borderline truths increased the perceived accuracy of those statements.[87]

Contemporary uses of information have had similar purposes of persuading mass publics. During the Cold War, the Soviet Union used disinformation campaigns, covert agents, and front organizations to seek to influence events abroad, including elections, through broadcasts or covert organizations, and financing. Former KGB officers who defected to the West have spoken of campaigns to undermine the United States and NATO.[88] The United States reciprocated with its own propaganda measures, and in the early Cold War established its first peacetime propaganda apparatus meant to craft and distribute messages intended to enhance perceptions of the United States. It did so by establishing Radio Free Europe in Munich to broadcast pro-Western messages into Eastern Europe as a "war of words" that might ultimately persuade those populaces of Western virtues.[89] These propaganda efforts operated alongside the vast spending on conventional and nuclear weapons.

Deploying information strategically – irrespective of the medium – operates on the premise that individuals can be persuaded. The notion is not fanciful. Most political debates are complex, and reasonable people can take either side of a debate. Individuals might all agree that the goal of racial equity, for example, but be ambivalent or conflicted about the optimal policy for achieving that end.[90] Foreign policy is ripe for this type of ambivalence. Individuals might agree on the goal of more peace, but internally debate the combination of defense spending, intervention, and alliance formation that will yield that goal. Consistent with the notion of ambivalence, John Zaller argued in 1992 that "individuals do not possess 'true attitudes,' in the usual technical sense of the term, on most political issues, but a series of considerations that are typically rather poorly integrated."[91] The assertion tracks closely with Sniderman and Piazza who point to "the pliability of the policy positions of substantial numbers" of individuals on particular policy positions, and their ability to "be dislodged from the positions they have taken on many issues … by calling their attention to countervailing considerations."[92]

---

[87] Gordon Pennycook, Tyrone Cannon, and David Rand, "Prior exposure increases perceived accuracy of fake news," *Journal of Experimental Psychology*, 147, 12 (2018), 1865–1880.

[88] Richard Schultz and Roy Godson, *Desinformatsia: Active Measures in Soviet Strategy* (Pergamon Press, 1984).i

[89] Garth Jowett and Victoria O'Donnell, *Propaganda and Persuasion* (Sage, 2006), 5; Melissa Feinberg, *Curtain of Lies: The Battle over Truth in Stalinist Eastern Europe* (Oxford University Press, 2017).

[90] R. Michael Alvarez and John Brehm, "Are Americans Ambivalent Towards Racial Policies?" *American Journal of Political Science*, 41, 2 (April 1997), 345–374.

[91] John Zaller, The Nature and Origins of Mass Opinion, (New York: Cambridge University Press, 1992), 308.

[92] Paul Sniderman and Thomas Piazza, *The Scar of Race* (Harvard University Press, 1993), 178.

Not only are policy issues complex, citizens often lack the information they need to make informed judgments on policies, a combination that has been referred to as a "democratic dilemma." To be sure, the citizens of a nondemocratic country also seek out information with which to inform their view about the wisdom of different policy choices, although those participatory ties are less robust in a nondemocracy than a democracy. In its strongest form, the process of democratic governance is predicated on the ability of citizens to make informed choices about policies, except "the complexity seems to impose intolerable information on people seeking to make informed choices" and policy tradeoffs.[93] An optimistic resolution of the democratic dilemma suggests that individuals turn to the media to acquire information that can help them suss out a reasonable policy position. The differential gains model illustrates that process of information acquisition, showing that news can help individuals process policy debates, and that the more news individuals consume, the greater their ability to distill the key issues and participate in the policy process.[94] Lupia and McCubbins are less sanguine, noting that the news environment exacerbates the democratic dilemma because it is flawed and therefore creates "a mismatch between the requirements of a democracy and most people's ability to meet these requirements."[95]

My argument builds on the differential gains model but positions it in the context of social media and differentiates on the basis of regime type. Figure 3 outlines the proposed mechanism through which individuals formulate preferences that inform political participation. The fainter arrow on the left previews the argument of this Section and Section 4: the influence of social media in a nondemocratic society is less concentrated than in a democracy. Underlying this logic is that individuals in a democracy typically have inchoate preferences on most foreign policy issues. They will either seek out information or be exposed to information that helps them negotiate or resolve topics they

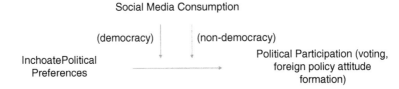

Figure 3 The role of social media as a moderator between political preferences and participation

---

[93] Lupia and McCubbins, *The Democratic Dilemma*, xi.
[94] Jinhee Kim and Ki Deuk Hyun, "Political Disagreement and Ambivalence in New Information Environments," *Telematics and Informatics*, 32, 8 (December 2017), 1586–1596.
[95] Lupia and McCubbins, *The Democratic Dilemma*, 1.

could decide either way. Social media is then central to the process of information acquisition.

Although scholars have increasingly noted that at least some types of non-democracies are responsive to public attitudes,[96] freedom of the media generally corresponds with regime type. Democracies tend to have a more open media environment – defined as media independence, self-censorship, and pluralism – than nondemocracies, where information is centralized, controlled, and censored.[97] The media environments within these regime types affect what Farrell and Schneider call "contested political knowledge," subjective facts such as the proper role of government in the economy, and "common political knowledge," which refers to agreed-upon political facts such as the way elections work. Nondemocracies have far fewer sources of contested knowledge – for example, normative debates about the proper functioning of government – than democracies.

Government control over the main media sources in an autocratic country limits the heterogeneity of news stories and perspectives. As Farrell and Schneider note, "there may be internal contestation between different factions within the elite, but such contestation is often clandestine, and is carefully insulated from the public realm, so as not to destabilize the shared expectations that anchor regime stability."[98] In other words, by setting the agenda, the media in an autocracy can shape the set of political issues seen as appropriate for contestation. On the types of topics that are viably contested, autocracies can ex post cut, control, or censor the supply of media if public attitudes animate and escalate.

The differential-gains model suggests that the democratic populace seeks information in the marketplace of ideas, in this case on social media. Social media can then influence political participation, by shifting the balance of support on an issue, shaping the type of political candidate that an individual supports, or by prompting an individual to show up at a campaign rally. A second-order effect is that social media can then affect the candidates that individuals choose to support, since elected officials go on to formulate foreign policy. It can affect the types of foreign policies that individuals would support, which affects the sustainability of foreign policy in a democracy.

Used for benign purposes, social media can indeed enhance democratic participation. Used for malicious purposes, however, the effect can be distortionary, exacerbating the mismatch between the aspirations of democratic engagement and citizens' ability to realize those aspirations, and creating the

---

[96] Jessica Weeks, "Strongmen and Straw Men: Authoritarian Regimes and the Initiation of International Conflict," *American Political Science Review*, 106, 29 (May 2012), 326–347.

[97] Reporters without Borders, https://rsf.org/en/detailed-methodology

[98] Henry Farrell and Bruce Schneider, *Common-Knowledge Attacks on Democracy*, Research Publication No. 2018-7 (October 2018), 9.

possibility of differential losses from media consumption. The assumption of the differential-gains model is that the marketplace of ideas is replete with more information and that this information is accurate. Social media fundamentally upends that assumption since the information that travels fastest and furthest on social media is misinformation. The differential-losses model I outline suggests a framework in which individuals go into the marketplace of ideas and rather than leaving more informed about a policy, they leaving confused, unwilling to believe what they read, distrusting of institutions, or further aggravated by the social or political "other." The next section outlines those potential ways that malicious actors might adversely affect smoothly functioning democratic governance.

Exploitation by Malicious Actors

The previous sections outline the theoretical differences between traditional and social media as well as the notion of a democratic dilemma wherein citizens seek out information. Propaganda is not new. As earlier sections suggested, actors have always acted as though they could deploy information strategically to effect political aims favorable to their perspective. What differs in the current media environment is that now actors can operate with ruthless efficiency. In the past, countries were required to conduct expensive training and risk the movement of spies transnationally. Joseph Nye notes that "now similar effects can be accomplished remotely at much lower cost. It is much easier to send electrons across borders than human agents."[99] Actors with nefarious aims can achieve similar ends but at lower costs because of the amplification effect of social media.

For malicious actors to opportunistically tilt the balance of support on an issue, paralyze individuals' thought processes, or intensify social or political divisions, however, requires an additional consideration. Social media must be relatively indefensible to actors who seek to use it as a weapon of war. As this section will outline, those trying to manipulate the technology to shape a narrative do have an offensive advantage that is difficult to counter. First, though, who are these malicious actors? Actors who have the potential and interest in misusing social media are of three types, according to research led by the ethical AI group, OpenAI:

1. Low-skilled, limited-resource actors who may be ideologically motivated or simply curious about their abilities. They may attempt to alter training data to bias a language model.

---

[99] Joseph Nye, *Protecting Democracy in an Era of Cyber Information War*, 3.

2. Actors with moderate programming skills and resources who are able and willing to build a malicious product, such as tools for webspam.
3. Advanced persistent threats (APTs): highly skilled and well-resourced groups, like state-sponsored actors, with a long-term agenda.[100]

All of these groups can have an impact on democratic consumption of knowledge via social media. For the purposes of this analysis, I focus on the third group because it is most likely to incorporate state-based groups of the type with the capacity to influence domestic and foreign affairs abroad. The others lack the capacity to have these effects.

The second question is where and how these groups insinuate themselves in the media consumption process. As Kenneth Lieberthal and Peter Singer argue, "the internet was designed to share information easily, not prevent its flow," which creates vulnerabilities that can be easily exploited. The point has been made in a military context, such as China vis-à-vis the United States[101] and the type of cyber espionage campaign that Russia carried out against Ukraine, luring Ukraine security services into responding to emails that leave their system vulnerable to exploitation.[102] Those military vulnerabilities endemic to the open architecture of the Internet[103] are all the more salient in a civilian context.

Social media platforms build entirely on the original ethos of the Internet, ARPANET, the Defense Department network that privileged content neutrality, free speech, and few impediments to the flow of information online. Section 230 of the Communication Decency Act made the source of objectionable information, not the networks, culpable, which is why spam emails proliferated, even if networks found ways to filter and authenticate dubious forms of messages. The default setting for the Internet in general and social networks in particular is openness, but as Russell Brandom observed, "abuse is everywhere and left to their own devices, malicious actors can easily make platforms unusable."[104] They can do so exactly because the Internet has been an open, unregulated, and user-driven experience. Indeed, the entire business model not only attracts user-generated content but polemics, which draw and hold users online. Relatedly, that exchanges on social media are multidirectional between and among users rather than one-way, from the publisher to the reader, not only privileges the

---

[100] https://d4mucfpksywv.cloudfront.net/papers/GPT_2_Report.pdf, 6.
[101] Kenneth Lieberthal and Peter W. Singer, *"Cybersecurity and U.S.–China Relations"* (Brookings Institution, 2012), 14.
[102] Benjamin Jensen, Brandon Valeriano, and Ryan Maness, "Fancy Bears and Digital Trolls: Cyber Strategy with a Russian Twist." *Journal of Strategic Studies*, (2019), 7.
[103] Ibid., 19.
[104] Russell Brandom, "We Have Abandoned Every Principle of the Free and Open Internet," *The Verge*, December 19, 2017.

user but also complicates gatekeeping of content. Identifying malicious users and content is not only a subjective affront to the premise of the open Internet, it is like finding a needle in a haystack. Platforms would need to patch every vulnerability, which is difficult if not impossible.

Since the 2016 United States Presidential Election, Facebook has been more active in disrupting "inauthentic accounts" that violate its requirement for being associated with actual individuals but its efforts to do so also expose its challenges. The company advertised that, in 2017, it had suspended 30,000 fake accounts prior to the French presidential election and removed 3,000 divisive ads targeting American voters, citing the months of work and cyber-forensics it had invested in identifying the accounts' association with the Russian Internet Research Agency. Given the enormous number of users globally, however, the number of suspended accounts is both relatively trivial but also reveals the difficulty of finding those needles in the haystack and therefore the opportunities for manipulation.[105] Twitter has faced similar problems. A study of 1.5 billion tweets showed that Twitter's fraud detection algorithm took a month longer to identify abusive tweeting than the two scholars who generated their own machine-learning software.[106] Twitter has claimed that fewer than 5 percent of its active users are fake, and fewer than 8.5 percent use automation tools such as bots or cyborgs, although these had included an estimated 50,000 automated accounts connected to the Russian government, which had occasioned the US Congress to pressure Twitter into targeting the inauthentic accounts.[107]

Beyond the sheer volume of traffic on social media, the algorithms – technical elements, logic, and analytics that determine which users see which content – are closely held but not a mystery and therefore easily manipulated. Companies monetize the social media experience by collecting data about individual preferences based on which links they click, what they buy, and how long they spend on particular sites. Facebook, for example, uses a sorting algorithm that provides posts with a "relevancy score," an indication of an individual's preference for a particular type of story, news, or person. It then uses a "prediction algorithm" – an amalgamation of several algorithms that takes into account hundreds of variables – that predicts whether an individual will like, comment, or share a post.[108] Having collected data about the demographics of users, and

---

[105] www.theverge.com/2018/4/3/17194518/facebook-suspends-russian-internet-research-agency-pages-accounts-instagram

[106] Andy Greenberg, "Twitter Still Can't Keep Up with its Flood of Junk Accounts, Study Finds," *Wired*, February 8, 2019.

[107] Craig Timberg and Elizabeth Dwoskin, "Twitter Is Sweeping Out Fake Accounts Like Never Before, Putting User Growth at Risk," *Washington Post*, July 6, 2018.

[108] Will Oremus, "Who Controls your Facebook Feed," *Slate*, Jan 3, 2016.

how those users have engaged prior content, companies invite advertisers to show ads specific to those classifications. In its most benign form, news organizations have been found to structure their video feeds in ways that they understand will privilege their organization's stories on the basis of an "algorithm tweak."[109]

That same algorithm, however, is susceptible to the effects of manipulative targeting. The business model is based not only on networking among like-minded people, but also on targeted advertising, which lends itself to persuasion.[110] If individuals add personal labels such as anti-Semitic phrases, for example, then social media algorithms reveal those labels when groups or individuals seek sympathetic voices. Facebook's automated ad-buying software, for example, has been known to target individuals using anti-Semitic phrases, which means greater efficiency in organizing for violent ends, such as right-wing extremism.[111] One Senate Intelligence Report released in December 2018 found that, in 2016, the Internet Research Agency used Facebook's ad platform to target not only African Americans but African Americans with interests specifically in black nationalism or incarceration. It had a different set of messaging for white conservatives, Hispanics, LGBT groups, and other groups to generate interest.[112] The Internet Research Agency was able to achieve a higher click-through rate – the percentage of people who visit a web page and access a hypertext link to a particular advertisement – than the average on Facebook, indicating that the group had successfully finessed the ability to reach well-defined audiences.[113]

Similarly, the degree of amplification that social media affords can produce what French President Emmanuel Macron called "democratic destabilization." He has first-hand exposure to those effects. Two days prior to the 2017 election, Macron's emails were the subject of an email hack, which produced 20,000 emails that were then posted to the anonymous message board, 4chan, problematically, however, with many of either erroneous translations from French or biased interpretations of the law. From there, alt-right activists posted on Twitter and, according to a study of 17 million tweets, bots engaged in an operation that

---

[109] Edson Tandoc, Jr and Julian Maitra, "News Organizations' Use of Native Videos on Facebook: Tweaking the Journalistic Field One Algorithm Change at a Time," *New Media and Society*, 20, 5 (2018), 1679–1697.

[110] Thomas Zeitzoff, "How Social Media is Changing Conflict," *Journal of Conflict Resolution*, (2017), 1–22, 3.

[111] Kurt Wagner, "Facebook's Reliance on Software Algorithms Keeps Getting the Company into Trouble," *Recode*, September 14, 2017.

[112] Philip Howard, Bharath Ganesh, and Dimitra Liotsiou, *The IRA, Social Media and Political Polarization in the United States, 2012–2018*; 18.

[113] Renee DiResta, Dr. Kris Shaffer, Becky Ruppel et al., *New Knowledge Disinformation Report White Paper*, 37.

produced a viral sharing of the leaks, in part because bots generated spikes in content that then propelled increases in human posts, producing a "cascade of disinformation."[114]

Malicious actors can also buy old Facebook accounts using others' credentials, circumventing detection. An entity with reasonable amounts of resources can then run thousands of accounts simultaneously. They then set up network proxies so that coordinated action is undetected. They can operate as those individuals and participate in group discussions either to drive traffic to third-party websites that are trying to generate revenue, or sow division within a society. Since Facebook allows users to join 6,000 groups, these accounts can then be used to generate revenue for third party companies, or, even less benignly, to promote extremism or affect the discourse on an already-divisive political topic.[115] In other words, relatively low-skilled actors with nefarious aims can manipulate social media algorithms for the potential purposes of amplifying divisive political messages.

In the wake of these episodes that erode credibility, platforms such as Facebook have sought to increase transparency, especially in the way it permits paid advertising. It added a "paid for by" disclosure that is well-intentioned, but an experiment carried out by journalists, revealed it to be easily manipulated. In one test, VICE news applied to buy fake ads, pretending to be the staff of American senators. Facebook approved all of the requests, including from groups such as the Ninja Turtles PAC that might seem obviously inauthentic. Had the journalists been foreign agents, they might have been in a position to exploit the pages for misinformation, pointing to the continued ways in which the platform is vulnerable to foreign interference in elections and, more generally, the divisiveness of the political landscape.[116]

What makes all of these advantages even more attractive is that they are accessible, affordable, and plausibly deniable. Department of Justice indictments revealed that the manipulation of American discourse through the Internet Research Agency had a budget of more than $12 million in 2017, which is less than one-tenth of the amount the United States government spends on Radio Free Europe/Radio Liberty, intended to be a source of news and information to regions where the free flow of information is either banned or not developed.[117] Online misinformation campaigns are inexpensive because

---

[114] Emilio Ferrara, "Disinformation and Social Bot Operations in the Run-Up to the 2017 French Presidential Election," *First Monday*, 2017, http://firstmonday.org/ojs/index.php/fm/article/view/8005/6516

[115] Author's interview with anonymous source, January 10, 2019.

[116] William Turton, "We Posed as 100 Senators to Run Ads on Facebook: Facebook Approved All of Them," *Vice News*, October 30, 2018.

[117] DiResta et al., *New Knowledge* report, 6. https://pressroom.rferl.org/p/6091.html

they require only a computer, a reasonably fast connection, and a few individuals who are relatively but not extremely tech savvy. As the teenagers in Macedonia showed, the barriers to entry are low, both in terms of skills and resources. Compared with traditional information operations budgets, the online campaigns point to the asymmetric advantages that accrue to actors with relatively few resources.[118]

Cost effectiveness was one of the initial incentives for Russia. In 1999, the Russian Minister of Defense acknowledged that Russia had sought but failed to catch up with the United States and its allies since the end of the Cold War. Instead, Russia would need to find "revolutionary paths" and "asymmetrical directions" for keeping pace with mismatched capabilities and did so through information warfare. In other words, recognizing that they had far fewer resources to spend on offense or defense than countries like the United States, Russia could instead invest in online misinformation campaigns to offset their financial asymmetries.[119]

Further, actors trying to engage in online misinformation can do so without overtly implicating the government, thereby reducing the risk of retaliation. Russia's sponsorship of disinformation campaigns offers a valuable lens into the virtues of the approach. Russia engages in a form of open secrecy, in which it denies a formal role, thereby signaling limited aims and installing impediments to retaliation.[120] By most accounts, Russia relies heavily on cyber troops installed in St. Petersburg, Russia, where the Internet Research Agency, which operates with at least the tacit endorsement of Russian authorities, engages in a concerted effort to produce content intended to inflame targeted parts of a political spectrum and undermine faith in domestic governance institutions.

As this section has argued, the Internet in general and social media in particular are inherently open and democratic in nature. Anyone can post. Traffic is overwhelming in both amount and direction. The business model is based on hyper-targeting, using users' online behavior to predict their spending or political patterns. These algorithms are no mystery, which means that malicious actors can manipulate those algorithms to drive traffic to divisive content and sow discord. Monitoring runs counter to the principles of openness but also presents enormous technical challenges given the comparatively small number of actors trying to do harm and the enormous pool of actors. It is because of this configuration of factors that social media became, as Senator Warner put it, the

---

[118] Bradshaw and Howard, Table 3, p.21.

[119] Pomerantsev, "Inside the Kremlin's hall of mirrors."

[120] Austin Carson, *Secret Wars: Covert Conflict in International Politics* (Princeton University Press, 2018), 39.

"Wild West." As Section 4 suggests, democracies have been wilder and more difficult to tame than nondemocracies in a world of social media.

4 The Democratic Disadvantage and Autocratic Advantage

In book VI of *Democracy in America,* Tocqueville wrote at length about the role of newspapers in democratic society. He observed in the 1830s:

> It is impossible to obtain the co-operation of any great number of them unless you can persuade every man whose help you require that his private interest obliges him voluntarily to unite his exertions to the exertions of all the others. This can be habitually and conveniently effected only by means of a newspaper; nothing but a newspaper can drop the same thought into a thousand minds at the same moment. A newspaper is an adviser that does not require to be sought, but that comes of its own accord and talks to you briefly every day of the commonwealth, without distracting you from your private affairs.

Newspapers, according to Tocqueville, were the basis of national and local freedom.[121] To this day, the role of the media and freedom of the press is thought to distinguish democracies from nondemocracies both in general and specifically in reference to the differences in how they fight wars. Indeed, even nondemocratic countries hold elections, even if those elections are not competitive. Even particular types of nondemocracies are responsive to their publics.[122] As Levitsky and Way show, competitive authoritarianism has become more prevalent. These hybrid regimes are less a "diminished" form of democracy than a diminished form of authoritarianism. They hold elections on a regular basis, those elections tend not to be plagued by rampant fraud, but one of the key distinctions is that the incumbent can control access to media, denying the opposition adequate or independent coverage and ensuring instead that the media is biased in favor of the incumbent. The government controls leading television and radio stations, prevents independence, and creates a media monopoly rather than contestation as envisioned by democratic theory.[123] These differences have enormous implications in terms of how the populace seeks information about policy choices and how malicious actors can exploit the modern media landscape in democracies versus nondemocracies.

---

[121] Alexis de Tocqueville, Democracy in America, 1835, Chapter VI.
[122] Barbara Geddes, Joseph Wright, and Erica Frantz, "Autocratic Breakdown and Regime Transitions: A New Data Set," Perspectives on Politics, 12, 2 (2014), 313-331.
[123] Steven Levitsky and Lucan Way, "Elections without Democracy: The Rise of Competitive Authoritarianism," *Journal of Democracy*, 13, 2 (Apr 2002), 51–65; 57–58; Sebastian Stier, "Democracy, Autocracy and the News: The Impact of Regime Type on Media Freedom," *Democratization*, 22, 7 (2015), 1273–1295.

In the context of war, it is this openness that democracies have long found to be a comparative advantage. In making their case for the advantages that democracies have in terms of selecting into "wiser" wars, Reiter and Stam observe that a marketplace of ideas can thrive in liberal democracies that have a free press. Unobstructed by government censorship, newspapers can expose unwise presidential pursuits, present the oppositional arguments, and weed out the foolish ideas via a populace now informed by the ideas and mobilized to express opposition.[124] They find that democracies are more likely to fight shorter and more successful wars than nondemocracies, corroborating other studies that have come to similar conclusions.[125]

The democratic advantage thesis has found its detractors, with critics questioning whether leaders lie, whether the press simply parrots support for incumbent positions, and whether the empirical record even supports the democratic triumphalism position.[126] The introduction of social media, the modern-day version of the newspaper that Tocqueville discussed, only draws the debate in sharper relief. Is the free press an asset or a curse when it comes to social media? Does regime type even matter and if so, how does a democratic populace and government accommodate, exploit, and defend itself in an era of social media compared to a nondemocracy? This section addresses those questions in the context of larger international relations debates about the differences between democracies and nondemocracies.

The Double-Edged Sword of the Democratic Free Press

Uncensored and unfiltered, the media enables leaders to communicate directly with the public and for the public to be informed on issues of foreign policy and galvanize against foolish foreign policies in ways that are impeded in a nondemocracy where the media is not free and the public is unable to adjudicate the advantages and disadvantages of a policy with relatively full information.[127]

In terms of direct communication between leaders and the populace, democratic leaders and organizations have indeed shown a propensity to use social media more than their nondemocratic counterparts. In a study of world leaders

---

[124] Reiter and Stam, Democracies at War, 23–24.

[125] David Lake, "Powerful Pacifists: Democratic States and War," *American Political Science Review*, 86, 1 (Mar 1992), 24–37.

[126] Michael Desch, "Democracy and Victory: Why Regime Type Hardly Matters," *International Security*, 27, 2 (Fall 2002), 5–47; Alexander Downes, "How Smart and Tough are Democracies? Reassessing Theories of Democratic Victory in War," *International Security*, 33, 4 (Spring 2009), 9–51; John Mearsheimer, *Why Leaders Lie: The Truth about Lying in International Politics* (Oxford University Press, 2013).

[127] Reiter and Stam, *Democracies at War*, 23.

who use Twitter and Facebook, Barberá and Zeitzoff found that 81 percent had active accounts, but that leaders in more democratic countries were more likely to rely on social media accounts for distributing content about their administration or government.[128] Twitter appears to be the tool of choice for most political elites, and is almost ubiquitous among highly democratic societies.

Campaigns have therefore offered an initial occasion for reliance on Twitter because they could help disseminate a political message that reaches broad audiences, help shape how voters see the candidate, offer opportunities to volunteer, and inform individuals about where to vote or attend a rally.[129] As a presidential candidate, John McCain had used the Internet for fundraising in 2000, but Barack Obama doubled-down and dramatically increased his embrace of social media in 2008. He joined Twitter in March 2007 and by the 2008 election was one of the most popular individuals to follow on Twitter. More than 118,000 followers followed his semi-weekly tweets, compared to 4,942 for his competitor John McCain.[130] By his re-election campaign in 2012, Twitter use had exploded and Obama's frequent tweeting (more than twice his competitors) was seen as the gold standard, almost a correlate of success, showing how the platform could be used to distribute pictures, videos, and campaign pitches.[131]

Increasingly, social media is more than just for campaigning, it is used to amplify the bully pulpit or political elite equivalent. In their analysis of Twitter as the most prevalent social media vehicle for communication, Parmelee and Bichard observe that "Politicians are always looking for ways to get their message across without having it filtered and potentially altered by others, such as news media. Twitter ... can fill that need."[132] As a prolific Twitter user, President Trump has touted the platform as a way to connect with his supporters: "Only the Fake News Media and Trump enemies want me to stop using Social Media (110 million people). Only way for me to get the truth out!"[133] Social media connects political elites with the public, and because of the bi- and multi-directionality of the exchange, brings the prospect of an exchange and feedback rather than simply a transmission of information.

---

[128] Pablo Barberá and Thomas Zeitzoff, "The New Public Address System: Why Do World Leaders Adopt Social Media?" *International Studies Quarterly*, 62, 1 (March 2018), 121–130.

[129] Andreas Jungherr, "Twitter Use in Election Campaigns: A Systematic Literature Review," *Journal of Information Technology and Politics*, 13, 1 (2016).

[130] Zoe Fox, "The Digital Smackdown: Obama 2008 vs Obama 2012," *Mashable*, September 23, 2012.

[131] Amelia Adams and Tina McCorkindale, "Dialogue and Transparency: A Content Analysis of How the 2012 Presidential Candidates Used Twitter," *Public Relations Review*, 39, 4 (Nov 2013), 357–359.

[132] John Parmelee and Shannon Bichard, Politics and the Twitter Revolution: How Tweets Influence the Relationship (Lexington Books, 2012), 12.

[133] https://twitter.com/realdonaldtrump/status/892383242535481344

For similar reasons – that social media acts as an amplifier – governments have invested in cyber troops as a form of public diplomacy, with countries connected through social media in ways that are endogeneous to the bilateral connectivity; for example, the United States is linked strongly to countries such as the United Kingdom, France, Mexico, and India, countries with whom it shares strong political or migratory connections.[134] The increased connectivity has provided a platform for governments to distribute their message, a vehicle for promoting a message globally and at relatively low cost. Just as almost all democratic leaders are on social media, government entities within these countries also have a presence intended to promote strategic objectives.

In 2017, the Alliance for Fort Gordon in Augusta, Georgia, launched a new Cyber District. US Senator David Purdue (D-GA) lauded the efforts, saying, "Georgia is on the front lines of training the next generation of cyber warriors. In the face of ever-evolving attacks, our nation must strengthen its defense capabilities to combat the constant asymmetric threats we face on a daily basis."[135] While the specifics of the district are vague,[136] Fort Gordon does maintain social media accounts that advertise the cyber training unit's accomplishments, which positions the district squarely in countries' trends toward armies of "cyber troops," which consist of "government, military, or political party teams committed to manipulating public opinion over social media."[137] The UK's 77th Brigade, a group dedicated to psychological and cyber operations – the production and distribution of viral videos – operates openly on Facebook.[138]

While the openness of democratic societies creates opportunities for leaders and organizations to communicate directly with their populaces, a contemporary feature of democracies like the United States and the United Kingdom is both the partisan polarization and, correspondingly – as both cause and effect – the enormous diversity of political perspectives represented in the free press. Selecting into politically congenial news is not peculiar to social media; people have already done that with television and traditional print media. What is new with social media is the hyper-targeted nature of content. Social media filters help curate the user experience, which means consumers view information selectively

---

[134] George Barnett, Weiai Wayne Xu, Jianxu Chu et al., *Government Information Quarterly*, 34, 1 (Jan 2017), 37–44.

[135] "Announcing the Effort Gordon Cyber District," www.prnewswire.com/news-releases/announcing-the-fort-gordon-cyber-district-300499089.html, August 3, 2017.

[136] Matt Gallagher, "Army of 01101111: The Making of a Cyber Battalion," *Wired*, March 27, 2018.

[137] Bradshaw and Howard, *Troops, Trolls and Troublemakers.*

[138] Dan Robitzski, "The British Army Has an Official Viral Content Division," *Futurism*, November 14, 2018.

because the algorithms have been developed based on previous click histories to target and tailor information that is most likely to be seen as interesting to that particular user. Algorithms can create a "filter bubble,"[139] in which individuals are selectively exposed and outside actors develop information precisely to exploit the process of curation.

Against the backdrop of polarization, partisan stories, and filter bubbles, malicious actors can upend democratic advantages. While a democratic citizenry is uniquely poised as an audience – a susceptible audience at that – the perpetrator need not be authoritarian, nor foreign. Recognizing the potentially consequential nature of how social media can be exploited, advocates of Senate candidate Doug Jones, from Alabama, carried out a social media experiment for his special election in 2017. The experiment attempted to employ tactics similar to Russia's interference in 2016, which entailed paying for advertising, promoting particular media stories on social media, and linking the opponent's campaign to Russian accounts. The group spent $100,000 and allegedly did not affect the outcome of the election, but as the candidate himself, who was not part of the effort, said, "We had no idea about any of this ... we had some pretty sophisticated ... software to kind of monitor those things." As with the Russian case, the Alabama election demonstrated the potential to influence election outcomes.[140]

Similarly, a group called Psy-Group, an Israeli private intelligence company whose slogan is "Shape Reality," is capitalizing on the premise – and indeed the company's tagline – that "reality is a matter of perception." Accordingly, the group sought to enter into the contested cognitive space and tilt the balance of public support in favor of their particular message or the candidate that favored their message. The group developed fake identities, gathered openly available intelligence on the users it intended to target, and crafted an influence campaign, a strategy scalable to small local elections and larger national elections. Distinguishing itself from illegally operating alternatives such as Black Cube, which more flagrantly operated illegally by relying on individuals using false identities and pretending to work for false firms,[141] Psy-Group claims to have operated in the legal gray zone by not appropriating real people for avatars and only clandestinely recording conversations in jurisdictions that do not require two-party consent.[142] Even if not technically

---

[139] Dominic Spohr, "Fake News and Ideological Polarization: Filter Bubbles and Selective Exposure on Social Media," *Business Information Review*, 34, 3 (2017), 150–160; 152–153.

[140] John Sharp, "Doug Jones says to investigate misleading effort that supported his campaign," *Alabama*.com, December 2018, www.al.com/news/2018/12/doug-jones-says-to-investigate-misleading-effort-that-supported-his-campaign.html?outputType=amp

[141] Ronan Farrow, "Israeli Operatives Who Aided Harvey Weinstein Collected Information on Former Obama Administration Officials," *New Yorker*, May 6, 2018.

[142] Adam Entous and Ronan Farrow, "Private Mossad for Hire," *New Yorker*, February 19/25, 2019.

illegal, the examples point to the nearly infinite number and nature of actors and therefore the inevitable vulnerability of a democratic populace and its institutions.

Taken together, this analysis suggests that democracies may be particularly vulnerable to the weaponization of social media. The openness of the media environment presents vulnerabilities that can be mitigated only by reducing the transparency or access that is part of what makes a democracy a democracy. Thus, defense is challenging. Offense, however, is also a challenge. The dilemma is emblematic of how to respond more generally to so-called gray-zone operations. Underlying the premise of gray-zone operations is that the attacker engages in unconventional force in ways unlikely to provoke a retaliatory move that would be escalatory. Perpetrators calculate that their involvement is plausibly deniable and that the costs of escalation are high and therefore likely to prohibit a response. Those calculations are not unreasonable. Multiple studies show that democratic audiences are not enthused about retaliating for what they see as low-level offenses such as election interference, online media meddling, or even more aggressive cyberattacks. Deterrence, however, hinges on the threat of costly and credible retaliation. Without public support, however, those threats of retaliation are not credible, meaning that the perpetrator can continue attacking with relative impunity.

Countries have faced similar security challenges in the online world more generally: how to defend, whether retaliation is plausible, and therefore how to deter attacks. In 2011, the United States International Strategy for Cyberspace asserted the "right to use all necessary means – diplomatic, informational, military, and economic" in retaliation for a cyberattack.[143] Yet it was always dubious that the threat of military force against a cyberattack was at all credible, not least because the public has expressed reluctance to respond with military force to any kind of cyberattack.[144] In an act of realism, the United States essentially conceded the futility of cyber deterrence when it abandoned the strategy of deterrence in 2018 and moved to one of persistent engagement in which the United States would "operate continuously below the threshold of armed conflict to weaken our institutions and gain strategic advantage."[145] Shifting from deterrence to persistent engagement, the United States has more consistently deployed computer code within Russia's electric grid to warn it of ways in which the United States will respond to

---

[143] David Alexander, "US Reserves Right to Meet Cyber Attack with Force," *Reuters*, November 15 2011.

[144] Sarah Kreps and Jacquelyn Schneider, "Escalation Firebreaks in the Cyber, Conventional, and Nuclear Domains: Moving Beyond Effects-Based Logics," Journal of Cybersecurity, 5, 1 (2019), https://academic.oup.com/cybersecurity/article/5/1/tyz007/5575971.

[145] US Cyber Command, "Command Vision for US Cyber Command," April 2018, www .cybercom.mil/Portals/56/Documents/USCYBERCOM%20Vision%20April%202018.pdf? ver=2018–06–14–152556-010, pg. 3.

Russia's online attacks in the United States, a "defend forward" approach that signals a willingness to impose costs.[146]

Democracies, as these examples suggest, may face peculiar challenges deterring threats because public support for retaliatory measures is both important yet missing. In contrast, as the next section suggests, autocracies have distinct advantages over the openness of democracies. Autocracies can leverage information control and quell popular passions. Democracies cannot do the same. Nor can they credibly threaten aggressive, overt government responses against offensive action in the social media realm. The policies of persistent engagement, putting perpetrators on notice with frequent "digital shots across the bow," will likely be the new normal.[147] Unknown is whether the approach can offset the autocratic advantages while also avoiding the escalation that neither side necessarily wants.

The Authoritarian Advantage

President Reagan predicted in 1989 that "the Goliath of totalitarianism will be brought down by the David of the microchip," suggesting that Silicon Valley was creating the tools that would help groups organize to overcome authoritarian rule.[148] Not long after, President Bill Clinton remarked that the Internet would liberalize Chinese politics and that the Communist party's ability to censor the Internet would have the same outcome as trying to "nail jello to the wall."[149] These remarks were grounded in a form of cyber utopianism, the belief that the Internet would be emancipatory.

Cyber utopianism is based on the assumption that the main impediment to success in popular protests is that the protesters cannot supply a critical mass to overthrow the Goliath of government. Governments have tanks and airplanes, which are well-suited to quashing popular revolts, as the experiences of 1956 in Hungary and 1968 in Prague revealed. The logic Reagan outlined implied that technology could empower popular protests in ways that would render even a Goliath impotent. One impediment to successful protests was the rational decision to be unwilling to step foot in the street for collective dissent because the first, outnumbered individuals would be extinguished by the far more powerful state. The logic is referred to as the rebel's dilemma, a rational reason for individuals to remain inert despite a collective interest in overthrowing

---

[146] David Sanger and Nicole Perlroth, "US Escalates Online Attacks on Russia's Power Grid," *The New York Times*, 15 June 2019.

[147] Ibid.

[148] Quoted in Barry Dumas, *Diving into the Bitstream: Information Technology Meets Society in a Digital Age*, 18.

[149] Quoted in Nye, *Protecting Democracy in an Era of Cyber Information War*, 1.

a state, for example.[150] Technology, according to the initial optimistic view of its potential, could resolve these collective action problems by helping individuals communicate and organize about the timing and location of protest activities where that information was previously unknown.[151] Steinert-Threlkeld shows empirically how social media can produce what he calls "spontaneous collective action," in which large numbers of people without any centralized leadership overcome the rebel's dilemma and engage in large-scale protest by coordinating through their online networks.[152]

Gradually, the cyber utopian belief that young, technology-savvy activists could overcome the power and influence of authoritarian leaders has been eclipsed by a less triumphal, more dystopian view: that the same attributes that make the Internet attractive for opponents can offer tools of repression.[153] Authoritarian governments may be responsive to the populace but nonetheless – or perhaps by consequence – seek to control those populations, and they seek ways to keep public opposition at bay. As Dunn observed, in a world of social media that can empower restive citizens, "revolutions will become impossible in conditions in which previously they would have been comparatively simple to bring about."[154] Authoritarian leaders furnish a media environment that seeks to conceal the basis of contested knowledge and minimize common political knowledge about group preferences, with a goal of ensuring regime survival.[155] Their overarching strategy is to create a sense of "pluralistic ignorance" in which the autocratic government seeks to manufacture a sense of support by cabining the perception of opposition,[156] but the government has a range of tools at their disposal for controlling social media in ways that maximize the prospects for regime survival. They can challenge online narratives, censor, or cut access altogether. Deibert et al. have organized these potential forms of control around a three-generation framework for thinking about how autocratic countries can use social media to prop up the regime.

The first generation was to find various ways to restrict or cut Internet access by way of limiting the organizing potential of dissidents. During the Egyptian uprising in 2011, protestors had initially been successful harnessing Facebook to organize mass protests until Egypt's leader. The government responded by

---

[150] Mark Irving Lichbach, *The Rebel's Dilemma* (University of Michigan Press, 1998), 3–4.

[151] Ibid., 51–52.

[152] Zachary Steinert-Threlkeld, "Spontaneous Collective Action: Peripheral Mobilization During the Arab Spring," *American Political Science Review*, 111, 2 (2017), 379–403; 379.

[153] Dumas, *Diving into the Bitstream*, 19; Evgeny Morozov, *The Net Delusion: The Dark Side of Internet*, 7, 278, 339.

[154] Quoted in Lichbach, *Rebel's Dilemma*, 52.

[155] Henry Farrell and Bruce Schneider, *Common-Knowledge Attacks on Democracy*, Research Publication No. 2018-7 (October 2018), 10.

[156] Ibid., 9.

censoring the posts, but hackers then used proxy computers to route messages through other countries and anonymize their data in ways that could circumvent the government censors. The group "We Rebuild" routed its messages through Sweden, which allowed the group to continue organizing protests. The government responded by blocking access to Facebook, Google, and other key Internet services in an effort to impede organization through social networks, although debate continues about whether the efforts were ultimately successful. People then switched to text messaging, until the government appeared to disable cellular towers. Even then, however, groups appeared to assemble in the streets regardless, having reached a critical mass and momentum that did not necessarily require sustainment via social media.[157] In Cameroon, the French-led government has blocked Internet access in the English-speaking parts of the country that have sought to organize protests.[158]

Another way authoritarian governments have tried to deracinate the online organizing potential of social media is to use social media itself to identify and eliminate the organizers. Not only does online use leave a paper trail, including location information, that governments can use forensically to identify and then locate activists, the state can also harness some of the same attributes that help activists organize – access and amplification – to crowdsource a search for adversaries. The Iranian government, for example, created an online surveillance center, a cyberarmy of hackers that challenge activists, and crowdsourced the forensics to identify protestors based on online pictures.[159] Vietnam similarly has a 10,000-person cyber unit that navigates the Internet looking for anti-government criticism, then imprisons dissidents. The proliferation of "toxic information" led it to pass a new cybersecurity law that prohibits anti-government comments on social media. It has registered complaints with Facebook for not removing pages critical of the state, with the primary concern being popular protests that could undermine the government.[160]

Autocratic countries may have these tools at their disposal, but the approach is also a sign of regime weakness. Having to cut Internet access is tantamount to admitting defeat. Hassanpour shows that in Egypt, the regime's Internet shutdown may actually have inflamed individuals and thereby increased

---

[157] "Arab Spring Anniversary: When Egypt Cut the Internet," *Al Jazeera*, January 25, 2016; Matt Richtel, "Egypt Cuts off Most Internet and Cell Service," *The New York Times*, January 28, 2011.

[158] Abdi Latif Dahir, "This Documentary Tells the Story of Africa's Longest Internet Shutdown," *Quartz*, August 6, 2018.

[159] Scott Shane, "Spotlight Again Falls on Web Tools and Change," *The New York Times*, January 29, 2011.

[160] James Hookway, "Facebook on Notice as Vietnam Tightens Grip on Social Media," *Wall Street Journal*, January 9, 2019.

mobilization.[161] Practices that are tantamount to cutting access, such as a daily tax on social media, have also been linked to a backfire effect. Boxell and Steinert-Threlkeld show that Uganda's daily tax actually caused an increase in observed protests by 47 percent.[162]

Countries have therefore engaged in a second type of intervention, censoring some online information rather than cutting or limiting it. China engages in massive online censorship, for example. China takes a number of steps to prevent social media from being used to foment popular protest. The government restricts content that reflects negatively on leaders or the state's authority, whether obviously prohibited content such as reference to the Tiananmen Square crackdown, but also more nuanced content such as an empty chair that signified a Chinese dissident unable to leave China to receive a Nobel prize. Technology companies, for example, that produce apps, know to self-censor and hire a specific cadre of individuals trained to prevent objectionable material from going online to ensure that their company stays on the right side of the law.[163]

The government itself acts as a further check and has created an elaborate censorship system for promoting regime stability. The government tolerates criticisms of the government, but censors content that would mobilize people in a way that might hint at organizing, overcoming the collective action problem, and threatening the regime. The government, for example, will censor searches of "today" and "tonight" on the anniversary of Tiananmen Square.[164] King et al. showed, through a large-scale random experiment and participant observation, that social media posts intending to overcome collective action in ways that threatened the regime were systematically vulnerable to government censorship compared to critical posts that did not imply any effort at organizing for change.[165] China's success in censorship depends on Internet forms being domestic (e.g., China's WeChat, a multipurpose social media platform). Most countries cannot engage in these practices because they use American social media firms such as Twitter, which the regime cannot arbitrarily or unilaterally censor.

Autocrats are therefore increasingly relying on third-generation approaches: the strategic use of social media is to use large volumes of individuals to

---

[161] Navid Hassanpour, "Media Disruption and Revolutionary Unrest: Evidence from Mubarak's Quasi-Experiment," *Journal of Political Communication*, 31, 1 (2014).

[162] Levi Boxell and Zachary Steinert-Threlkeld, "Taxing Dissent: The Impact of a Social Media Tax in Uganda," https://arxiv.org/abs/1909.04107

[163] Li Yuan, "Learning China's Forbidden History, So They Can Censor It," *The New York Times*, January 2, 2019.

[164] Didi Kirsten Tatlow, "Censored in China," *The New York Times*, June 4, 2013.

[165] Gary King, Jennifer Pan, and Margaret Roberts, "Reverse-Engineering Censorship in China: Randomized Experimentation and Participant Observation," *Science*, August 22, 2014.

participate in online discussions in order to craft a pro-regime narrative. Even nondemocracies have incentives to be seen allowing some degree of discussion, but they also have incentives to stymie large-scale protests. One way they have tried to finagle that balance is through the use of troll farms to shape discourse either in favor of the government and its policies. Munger et al refer to this as "soft censorship" – the regime essentially floods social media with messages congenial to itself, antagonistic to an opposition, the goal being to promote a pro-regime narrative among the populace. Russia, Venezuela, and China all practice some form of soft censorship.[166]

Analogous to Russia targeting contested knowledge in a democratic society, its Internet Research Agency seeks to manipulate opinion in its own country. In some cases, the troll farms promote perhaps unrealistically clean or tranquil images of Russia in ways that indirectly endorse Putin as the incumbent leader of the country.[167] Just as citizens abroad do not know to put their defenses up because they are simply coming into contact with information, domestic audiences might view the barrage of pro-Kremlin news in their social media feed without affront, or view crude dialogue purveyed by trolls as characteristic of contemporary political debate and less easily dismissed. The effect of troll interventions is not necessarily homogeneous. One study found that trolls have been more effective at causing online discussions to detour from politics, but that discussions of poor economic growth or high unemployment are relatively stubborn, not prone to distractions.[168]

In Venezuela, the ruling Maduro party has also used third-generation tactics to try to undermine social media coordination for protests. Access to social media in general and Twitter in particular is fairly high but rather than shut down access, the ruling party has tried to use social media to distract the protesters. During major protests, the regime discusses far more topics on a daily basis than in periods of nonprotest, whereas protesters' points of discussion during protests are focused almost exclusively on those protests compared to during other periods. Munger et al. show that the regime favored "'discourse-structuring' hashtags during the protest, each of which was designed to develop a conversation unrelated to the talking points of *La Salida*."[169]

---

[166] Kevin Munger, Richard Bonneau, Jonathan Nagler, and Joshua Tucker, "Elites Tweet to Get Feet off the Streets: Measuring Regime Social Media Strategies during Protest," *Political Science Research and Methods*, 7, 4 (October 2019), 815–834.

[167] www.theverge.com/2018/4/3/17194518/facebook-suspends-russian-internet-research-agency-pages-accounts-instagram

[168] Anton Sobolev, "How Pro-government 'Trolls' Influence Online Conversations in Russia," www.wpsanet.org/papers/docs/2019W-Feb-Anton-Sobolev-Trolls-VA.pdf

[169] Munger et al., "Elites Tweet," 829.

Similarly, China has embraced third-generation approaches, but an enormously scaled-up version. The government famously employs what has become known as the fifty-cent party, or fifty-cent army, government-sponsored commentators rumored to make fifty ents for every message they post online. Their strategy is to troll readers so they experience outrage toward the poster, which is thought to deflect negativity toward the regime. Distracted by their new rage toward the individual, the hope is that they forget any misdeeds by the government.[170] The point of the nearly 448 million annual posts is not to engage in vitriol or debate, merely to "distract and redirect public attention from discussions or events with collective action potential."[171]

In Myanmar, the Tadmadaw, the name given to the armed forces that operates autonomously from the civilian part of the government, was associated with using social media to spread misinformation about the minority Rohingya. The Tadmadaw, which allegedly went to Russia to learn programming, hacking, and psychological warfare, is the source of approximately "two-thirds of hate speech, hoaxes, and vitriol" in the country.[172] In its initial social media pursuits, the military set up news pages on benign, unrelated topics such as music and celebrities. Those pages then became the site of inflammatory content – such as fabricated images of corpses that they attributed to the Rohingya – beginning in about 2013. As the user base burgeoned to 18 million people, the capacity for collective action increased. In 2014, rumors posted on Facebook about a Muslim man raping a Buddhist woman led to lethal riots. A couple of years later, the military began using Facebook to disseminate rumors that Buddhist monks were organizing anti-Muslim protests and that an attack was imminent.[173] In March 2018, the chairman of the UN Independent International Fact-Finding Mission on Myanmar concluded that the use of Facebook "had substantially contributed to the level of acrimony and dissension and conflict" that led to the ethnic cleansing of Rohingya Muslims.[174]

As the preceding sections suggest, the process of information acquisition that allows citizens to evaluate policies increasingly brings individuals into contact with news via social media. The content that spreads furthest and fastest is not always accurate, which means that the process of information acquisition is increasingly contaminated or at least distorted by exposure to social media. That

---

[170] Bradshaw and Howard, "Troops, Trolls and Troublemakers."

[171] Gary King, Jennifer Pan, and Margaret Roberts, "How the Chinese Government Fabricates Social Media Posts for Strategic Distraction."

[172] Paul Mozur, "A Genocide Incited on Facebook, with Posts from Myanmar's Military," *The New York Times*, October 15, 2018, https://twitter.com/paulmozur/status/1051867130801483778

[173] Ibid.

[174] Tom Miles, "UN Investigators Cite Facebook Role in Myanmar Crisis," *Reuters*, March 12, 2018.

the process of information acquisition is open to foreign actors introduces the prospect for using social media as a weapon of war. Democracies are much more susceptible to foreign distortion, however, because the marketplace of ideas is, by definition, unmediated and unfiltered. Autocracies, which were initially thought to be vulnerable to the diffusion of social media technology, have found ways to insulate themselves from the ways citizens can use social media to organize protests. Thus, whereas the open marketplace of ideas has long favored democracies, the rise of social media and ability of autocracies to disproportionately or more effectively respond to that rise, appears to be yielding the floor to autocracies.

The extent to which social media actually distorts individual decision-making and policy processing in a democracy is an empirical question. One of the most pessimistic perspectives originated from the Facebook CEO himself, who indicated that 126 million Americans saw Russian-backed fake news stories on Facebook. Consistent with this pessimism, another datapoint suggested that the twenty most popular fake news stories generated more engagement than the top twenty most popular real news stories, suggesting that the fake news was traveling further and faster than the truth. Citing these numbers, Zuckerberg reversed his earlier dismissal that "misinformation on Facebook changed the outcome of the election."[175]

A more optimistic perspective suggests that citizens come into contact with relatively little fake news. In a study of fake news exposure, Nyhan et al. found that just 27 percent of Americans visited fake news sites – defined as sites that published false or misleading claims in ways that favored a particular candidate – prior to the 2016 election. Those sites were just 2 percent of the information people consumed, and fake news exposure continues to decline.[176] Even if exposure is high, political persuasion is difficult, especially in a polarized world. Section 5 further interrogates the debate about fake news exposure on social media in its crosshairs. It does so less by looking back and taking stock for what people saw and the effect for that exposure, and more by offering a forward-looking study that examines new tools in online manipulation and the effect on political behavior.

5 Assessing the Impact of Social Media Manipulation

The case of Russian manipulation of social media in the 2016 election offers a visible and concrete study of how governments can use the openness of these platforms for malicious purposes. Mueller reported that foreign interference in

---

[175] Olivia Solon and Sabrina Siddiqui, "Russian-Backed Facebook Posts 'Reached 126m Americans' during US Election," *The Guardian*, October 30, 2017.

[176] Brendan Nyhan, "Why Fears of Fake News Are Overhyped," *Medium*, February 4, 2019.

American elections is the new normal. But what is the effect on political behavior, specifically, attitudes about key foreign policy issues? How do emerging technologies change how individuals interact with their news and what is the effect on trust in institutions? As the reach of social media has expanded, scholars have sought to understand the consequences for a range of attitudes and political behaviors. Yet as Lazer et al. note in *Science*, "there is little research focused on fake news and no comprehensive data-collection system to provide a dynamic understanding of how pervasive systems of fake news provision are evolving."[177] Moreover, there is no systematic evidence as to whether or how these emerging technologies might influence the public, whether creating confusion or shaping political beliefs.

This section proceeds by looking at the existing literature on the behavioral consequences of new media, both in terms of general social contagion and then in terms of political behavior. To date, however, studies of the foreign policy consequences of social media have been limited. To study how malicious actors might use social media for political purposes, I carried out experiments that used a natural-language processing (NLP) model called GPT-2 to manufacture news stories. OpenAI, an AI research group, has developed and released GPT-2 as a text prediction software that can both facilitate human creativity but also be a partner to fake news. Through a collaboration with OpenAI, I collected GPT-2–generated data to assess the potential for malicious actors to conduct misinformation in a democratic marketplace of ideas.

If malicious actors can generate credible news stories at scale, then the prospect for foreign influence in domestic affairs is high. Synthetic news stories, amplified through social media, can influence political debate, intensify social conflict, and affect the type of political candidates that the public is likely to support. Perhaps even more fundamentally, the proliferation of synthetic news can undermine trust in the democratic process if the public comes to distrust the news they read. On the other hand, if malicious actors have the tools to generate news stories at scale, but the public can reliably discern the synthetic from the real, then the advent of these technologies poses little threat to democratic governance and concerns about the proliferation are unwarranted.

Whether humans can detect computer- versus human-generated text has enormous implications for both foreign election interference and debates about regulation. Trying to deflect calls for greater regulation, in

---

[177] David Lazer, Matthew Baum, Yochai Benkler et al., "The Science of Fake News," *Science*, 359 6380, March 9, 2018; 1094–1096; 1096.

October 2019, Mark Zuckerberg said that the public should be trusted as the arbiter of authentic content.[178]

This analysis shows that individuals overwhelmingly find that the synthetic text is authentic and cannot distinguish between the AI- and human-generated text, evidence that does not augur well for hopes that the public can judge what is credible. It also shows that the synthetically generated news does not actually change people's minds on foreign policy issues, although insights into foreign-conducted misinformation campaigns suggests that the goal is not actually to change minds but rather to confuse and muddy the waters, eroding trust in institutions because individuals can no longer believe what they read. In this sense, the experiments confirm that new AI tools can help malicious actors succeed in those campaigns. On the other hand, many respondents can point to dubious aspects of the text, suggesting that media literacy campaigns that educate the public about the attributes of fake text might be effective.

Existing Research on the Behavioral Consequences of New Media

In a landmark study conducted by Facebook, researchers investigated how the structure of the news feed or content affected individual attitudes, specifically their emotional state. Individuals were shown either positive or negative stories in their feed, and by the end of the week, their own posts corresponded with the sentiment to which they had been exposed. Although the study was conducted on questionable ethical standards, insofar as it did not solicit individual approval for stimuli that in some cases were negative and melancholy-inducing, the experiment did show that by manipulating the sentiment to which more than 680,000 users were exposed, they could affect – through emotional contagion – those individuals' moods and follow-on actions such as participation in political protests.[179]

A number of studies have demonstrated the contagion effects of social media across contexts.[180]

One study showed that rainfall can affect emotional sentiment not just of the individuals directly affected but those connected online, manifested as changes in the emotional content of messages across people within the same social

---

[178] "Facebook's Mark Zuckerberg: Private Companies Should Not Censor Politicians," *CNN*, October 18, 2019.

[179] Adam Kramer, Jamie Guillory, and Jeffrey Hancock, "Experimental Evidence of Massive-Scale Emotional Contagion through Social Networks," *Proceedings of the National Academy of Sciences of the United States of America*, 2014.

[180] Johan Ugander, Lars Backstrom, Cameron Marlow, and Jon Kleinberg, "Structural Diversity in Social Contagion," *PNAS*, April 17, 2012; 109 (16), 5962–5966.

network.[181] Another showed the diffusion of emotions online, such that negative posts, for example, were more likely to follow from an over-exposure to
negative content.[182]

That online engagement would produce offline political participation is not
a foregone conclusion. Indeed, it could plausibly contribute to "slacktivism,"
the sense that posting a political message on Facebook is a substitute for
political behavior in the form of offline activism or voting.[183] Yet it corroborates
other studies that found a correlation between political behavior on and offline,
suggesting that those who feel strongly enough to post and read online are then
also impelled to engage offline.[184]

In terms of political behavior, one prominent randomized control trial of
61 million Facebook users during the 2010 congressional elections tested the
way online social networks operate, as well as the mimetic effects of behavior
within networks. Messages that indicated that individuals had voted had
a notable increase in voting participation compared to those who did not see
that message. The "I Vote" message took the form of virtue signaling that
impelled others in the network to vote as well, suggesting that social networks
have powerful effects on key forms of political behavior such as voting.[185]

Despite the volume of research on the impact of Facebook on political
behavior, the extension to foreign policy behavior has been limited. Existing
research points in the direction that impacts might run, however. Kertzer and
Zeitzoff show, for example, that social group cues influence individuals, either
implicitly or explicitly pushing social conformity. They do so by providing
credible information to groups, tantamount to a second opinion about an issue
such as war and peace on which the modal individual is bereft of political
knowledge.[186] Public attitudes then can put bottom-up pressure on leaders to
conform with individual preferences. Social media intensifies the strength of
social cues in part because of the way it amplifies posts.

---

[181] Lorenzo Coviello, Yunkyu Sohn, Adam Kramer et al., "Detecting Emotional Contagion in Massive Social Networks," *PLOS One*, March 12, 2014.

[182] Emilio Ferrara and Zeyao Yang, "Measuring Emotional Contagion in Social Media," *PLOS ONE*, November 6, 2015.

[183] Jessica Vitak, Paul Zube, Andrew Smock, Caleb Carr, Nicole Ellison, and Cliff Lampe, "It's Complicated: Facebook Users' Political Participation in the 2008 Election," *Cyberpsychology, Behavior, and Social Networking*, 14, 3 (2011), 107–113.

[184] Meredith Conroy, Jessica Feezell, and Mario Guerrero, "Facebook and Political Engagement: A Study of Online Political Group Membership and Offline Political Engagement," *Computers in Human Behavior*, 28 (2012), 1535–1546.

[185] Robert Bond, Christopher Fariss, Jason Jones et al., "A 61-million-person experiment in social influence and political mobilization," *Nature*, 489 (2012), 295–298.

[186] Joshua Kertzer and Thomas Zeitzoff, "A Bottom-Up Theory of Public Opinion about Foreign Policy," *American Journal of Political Science*, 61, 3 (2017), 543–558.

There are other theoretical ways social media can affect foreign policy. In a traditional media context, with media sources such as newspaper or television, the symmetry of information between leaders' understanding of events on the ground and that of the populace takes time to converge.[187] The temporary asymmetry between leaders and the public about the events in wartime privileges leaders up to the point where information available to the public converges more closely with that of elites. Those informational advantages that accrue to leaders make reality "elastic" for the public.[188] Baum and Potter note that "social media sometimes can . . . narrow the elasticity of reality and potentially speed up its collapse by pushing more information into the information marketplace more rapidly than was possible in the traditional media environment."[189] Other times, however, it can create a reality so elastic that the public no longer trusts what it hears, which has important implications for the ways that foreign governments can influence political debates abroad. Conflict is ultimately a political act and the manipulation of the media environment can serve as a vehicle of influence.

Actors trying to influence foreign media environments for strategic gain have operated via two different avenues. One has focused on promoting pro-government messages on social media. Russia propaganda on social media typically targets the near abroad (Baltic states, Ukraine, Moldova, and Belarus) to foster viewpoints that are sympathetic to Russian positions; for example, amenability to Russia's incursions into Ukraine. China, like Russia, underwrites a large group of internet commentators meant to manipulate opinion in ways favorable to China, a massive operation that has culminated in almost 500 million posts on China-based social media. Rather than engaging in divisive issues, however, their aim is intended to change the subject away from controversy, particularly the type that might reflect negatively on the regime, and toward more benign topics.[190]

A second way is to engender policy paralysis and erode trust in institutions further afield (e.g., in the United States, France, and the United Kingdom). This is done by flooding news sites with content that is either misleading or polemical in ways that aim to exploit divisions on contentious issues.[191] Examples

---

[187] Matthew Baum and Philip Potter, "The Relationships between Mass Media, Public Opinion, and Foreign Policy: Toward a Theoretical Synthesis," *Annual Review of Political Science*. 2008. 11: 39–65.

[188] Matthew Baum and Tim Groeling, "Reality Asserts Itself: Public Opinion on Iraq and the Elasticity of Reality," *International Organization*, Vol. 63, no. 3 (July 2010), 443-479.

[189] Baum and Potter, "Media, Public Opinion, and Foreign Policy,"

[190] King et al., "How the Chinese Government Fabricates Social Media Posts."

[191] Todd Helmus, Elizabeth Bodine-Baron, Andrew Radin et al., *Russian Social Media Influence* (Rand Corporation, 2018), x-xii.

include the Russian news service RT weighing in on the NFL national anthem controversy or vaccine debates by promoting and amplifying the most polarizing positions in those debates.[192] Even if the information is not actually patently wrong, it is divisive and is intended to erode trust in institutions. The question is the extent to which these efforts have reverberated through society.

Evidence suggests that one consequence may be a version of nihilism, individuals come to believe nothing individuals have increasingly discounted what they read online. In 2019, Pew Research Center found that 50% of Americans see made-up news and information distributed on social media as a "very big problem in the country today," more than the percentage of people who ranked violent crime, climate change, racism, immigration, terrorism, and sexism as big problems. In the same poll, 68% of Americans reported that the distribution of fake news has eroded confidence in the government, 54% agreed that it had negatively impacted confidence in each other, and 51% in political leaders' ability to get work done. While only 38% of Americans think they have come across fake news, most have nonetheless changed their acquisition of news, with 63% saying they no longer obtain news from a particular outlet, 52% saying they use social media differently, and 43% lessening their overall news intake. The evidence suggests a backlash effect in which the process of news acquisition has brought some degree of contact with fake news, which has the effect of reducing political awareness and eroding the foundations on which democratic governance relies.

Perhaps even more pernicious, almost half of Americans report that they stopped interacting with certain people that they expect might introduce fake news into the conversation. Here again, however, the increasing tendency to retreat to self-selected groupings is counterproductive for societal cohesion since it is closer associations across groups that create social capital and dampen divisions.[193] The prospect for a vicious cycle or negative feedback loop therefore emerges. Preexisting polarization creates an opportunity for social media disinformation, which then creates distrust, social retreat, more polarization, and greater potential effects for disinformation.

The distrust goes well beyond the United States. Only 10% of Canadians say they have not fallen for fake news, and a corresponding 89% said in 2019 that they did not trust social media companies (up from 81% in 2018), several points higher than the percentage of Canadians who report distrust of cybercriminals (85%), even though cybercrime is often cited as one of Canadians' most

---

[192] *Countering Russian Information Operations in the Age of Social Media*, Council on Foreign Relations, 21 November 2017, www.cfr.org/report/countering-russian-information-operations-age-social-media

[193] Robert Putnam, *Bowling Alone: America's Declining Social Capital* (Simon and Schuster, 2000).

significant concerns. Most Canadians (65%) blame Facebook, 62% cited "the Internet" and 49% YouTube, whereas television was blamed by 4% of Canadians and print media only 35%. Nonetheless, 58% of Canadians think that fake news on social media has negatively impacted political debates.[194]

Cross-national evidence is mixed in terms of the net effects of social media. Figure 4 shows these crosscutting currents when it comes to the effects of social media, with publics seeing both virtues and vices. On one hand, individuals across many countries indicate that their social media use overwhelmingly makes them more likely to participate in political debates, and political participation is a cornerstone of democracy. On the other hand, individuals invariably agree that social media has made it easier to manipulate attitudes with false information and rumors, while also making the populace more divided in their opinions about politics. Only in a few countries does a minority of the population (41 percent) agree that social media has made society more divided, which is no coincidence given that Vietnam's access to social media has been controlled by the government.[195]

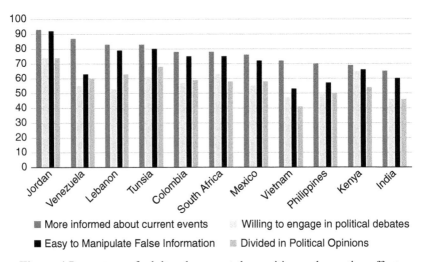

Figure 4 Percentage of adults who report the positive and negative effects of social media. Source: Pew Research Center.[196]

---

[194] Elizabeth Thompson, "Poll Finds 90% of Canadians Have Fallen for Fake News," *CBC*, June 11, 2019.

[195] "Vietnam Wants 50% of Social Media on Domestic Platforms by 2020," *Reuters*, November 8, 2018.

[196] "Publics in Emerging Economies Worry Social Media Sow Division, Even as They Offer New Chances for Political Engagement," *Pew Research*, May 13, 2019.

Whether, short of government censorship, the negative effects of social media can be countered is an empirical question. One argument suggests that education rather than regulation is the appropriate solution, given that regulation can – as the next section suggests – actually filter out content in imperfect and ideological ways that border on free-speech prohibitions. Media literacy indexes gauge countries' resilience to disinformation, measured by freedom of the press, reading, scientific and mathematical literacy, and levels of education. Finland scored the highest, followed by Denmark and the Netherlands.[197] Corroborating Finland's solid media literacy index, a team of researchers at Stanford's History Education Group gave social media posts to high school students in the United States and Finland and found that compared to the "bleak" performance of the Americans, the students in Finland had demonstrated "consistently superior outcomes" on identifying critical thinking in how they approached social media stories.[198]

Can Misinformation Succeed?

The preceding evidence suggests that the public decreasingly trusts what it reads online. If this is true, then the prospect of deep fakes or maliciously generated and distributed news articles should not be cause for concern. Individuals will easily cast what they read into the "fake news" bin. On the other hand, studies of viral news stories suggest that particular types of "affect" are more likely to be shared and magnified irrespective of their veracity. Some stories that have gone viral on social media seem flagrantly false or at least dubious, including some on satirical websites that advertise "because you love being lied to!" Under the heading of plausible-but-unlikely, the number six most engaged fake news story in 2018 (captured by the number of Facebook engagements) was about a man arrested for tranquilizing and raping alligators.[199] One of these was advertised as false, the other seemed distinctly unlikely, but both went viral in ways that reached recipients who may have been less informed – and therefore more credulous – about the source and veracity. As suggested earlier, truthfulness

---

[197] *Common Sense Wanted: Resilience to 'Post-Truth' and its predictors in the new Media Literacy Index 2018,* Open Society Institute, March 2018, www.rcmediafreedom.eu/Publications/Reports/Common-sense-wanted.-Resilience-to-post-truth-and-its-predictors-in-the-new-Media-Literacy-Index-2018

[198] Annabelle Timsit, "A Study Compared Finnish and American Students' Ability to Detect Fake News," *Quartz,* May 3, 2019.

[199] www.socialmediatoday.com/news/the-top-10-fake-news-articles-on-facebook-in-2018-info graphic/545165/

has little to do with virality. Moreover, research has shown that fake news flags or fact checks rarely reach their audiences.[200]

While online misinformation has become a constant, the ways that malicious actors might promote misinformation continue to change. The reason is that technologies improve that make fake news harder to detect. A 2019 US Senate report on foreign interference in US elections warned that Russian efforts to interfere are becoming "more sophisticated." One of the ways that malicious actors are trying to exploit the online media environment is through deep fakes, often the work of neural nets that rely on large amounts of data to manufacture reality. As Tarrow notes, "While such deceptions are at least annoying (and at most devastating), the real danger is that, through their diffusion and amplification, deep fakes feed into the psychological tendency human beings have to attend to negative images and thereby erode belief in the reliability of public discourse."[201] They are at their most devastating when they help a foreign government distort discourse in ways that might affect political behavior, such as vote choice that percolates up into decisions about the country's president, which in turn has enormous implications for foreign policy. Although the debate continues about whether exposure to fake news ultimately affected the 2016 presidential outcome, the fact is that a nontrivial fraction of the population was exposed and that malicious actors are continuing to devise stealthier ways to manipulate discourse.

To date, one limitation of fake news generation has been sheer human bandwidth and resources. Individuals working in the Internet Research Agency, for example, must generate new content by hand. They cannot post recycled or plagiarized material, which would easily trigger detection. New technologies, such as natural-language processing (NLP) models, can alleviate the resource burden by providing a large-scale text-generation tool. One of the most powerful models is called GPT-2, created by the research group OpenAI, cofounded by Elon Musk to promote ethical AI research. The ability of GPT-2 to predict text with nuance is based on a machine learning algorithm trained on 8 million websites, specifically on highly rated Reddit links, a proxy for whether the reader viewed the information as credible or edifying in ways that should theoretically increase data quality for GPT-2. The tool uses a recurrent neural network design developed by Google called the Transformer, which processes language by aggregating information from surrounding words to learn the

---

[200] Andrew Guess, Brendan Nyhan, and Jason Reifler, "Exposure to untrustworthy website in the 2016 US election," *Nature Human Behavior* (2020), https://www.nature.com/articles/s41562-020-0833-x?proof=trueMay%252F

[201] As Tarrow notes, fabrication – whether of text, images, or video – is just one modality of deep fake technology but is the one we focus on in this analysis because it is, as Tarrow concludes, the most dangerous because it goes beyond manipulation and is outright manufactured disinformation. Sidney Tarrow, "Lies, Fakes, and Deep Fakes," *Eurozine*, October 24, 2019.

meaning of those words and their context.[202] For example, words like "bank" can mean either the side of a river or a place that holds money. The neural networks process language to model the relationship between words in a sentence irrespective of where they are in the sentence. Attention scores disambiguate by giving "river" a high score if it is around "bank," weights based on context.[203]

The model works by users providing a prompt, whether words, sentences, headlines, or passages from an article and GPT-2 predicts the next words of the passage, mimicking the style and substance of the prompt, including the genre, whether poem, article, or policy memo. Aware of the potential for misuse, or aiming to understand the potential uses of the language model, OpenAI staggered the release of its models, starting with the smallest model in February 2019 and larger models incrementally in the subsequent months. These models are referred to as 124M, 355M, 774M, and 1.5B parameter models, sizes that approximate their power.[204] The decision to stage the release was based on concerns about the potential for misuse. As one headline put it, "Elon Musk's OpenAI Builds Artificial Intelligence So Powerful It Must Be Kept Locked Up for the Good of Humanity."[205] As the not-so-complimentary headline implied, some parts of the AI community were other than enthused about the staged release, implying that it was the opposite of OpenAI's stated transparency goal. In defense of the approach, OpenAI insisted on anticipating and understanding the potential uses prior to release, collaborating with other institutions and scholars to study those potential impacts. The empirical analysis presented here is a product of that collaboration.

The goal of the research was to study a plausible use case for AI-generated text. One such case involves a foreign government overcoming human text-generating capabilities by feeding online news snippets into an NLP model such as GPT-2 and producing fake news in large quantities, essentially clogging the media with a cacophony of information that clouds reality. At best, individuals might become so confused that they do not believe anything they read, distrusting the media altogether and thereby complicating the process of governance – including of foreign policy – which requires shared reference points or basic agreements about truthfulness.[206] At worst, individuals might stop believing

---

[202] Ashish Vaswani, Noam Shazeer, Niki Parmar et al., "Attention Is All You Need," https://arxiv.org/abs/1706.03762

[203] https://ai.googleblog.com/2017/08/transformer-novel-neural-network.html

[204] OpenAI released the medium parameter model (355M) in May 2019, large (774M) in August 2019, and full (1.5B) in October 2019.

[205] Jasper Hamill, "Elon Musk-Founded OpenAI Builds AI So Powerful It Must Be Kept Locked Up for the Good of Humanity," *Metro UK*, February 15, 2019.

[206] Sarah Kreps and Miles McCain, "Not Your Father's Bots," *Foreign Affairs*; Sabrina Tavernise and Aidan Gardiner, "'No One Believes Anything': Voters Worn Out by a Fog of Political News," *The New York Times*, November 18, 2019.

anything other than what confirms their priors, which likely means their partisan elites, which is likely to exacerbate polarization and the pendulum of foreign policy swings from party to party.

To analyze the potential for the misuse of synthetic text, I ran a series of experiments.[207] Because the research aim was to understand when AI-generated misinformation would be indistinguishable from real news and therefore able to confound the public's information environment, I focused on the public's perception of foreign policy events in the media. Malicious actors have a range of ways they might try to meddle with domestic foreign policy debates, even within the context of social media, but since one of the standard approaches is through misinformation via manufactured news stories, I focused on manufactured content in the form of current foreign policy events.

The first experiment tested the utility of AI-generated text by comparing three different size models: 345M parameter, 774M parameter, and 1.5B parameter models, which correspond to the capacity and power of the models.[208] The objective was to study whether increases in model size increased quality of the output, operationalized in this case by whether the outputs come to approximate the credibility of the real news source on which they are based. To test the potential utility of these new NLP tools, I generated a set of news stories based on an original *New York Times* article about the North Korean nuclear program. I chose the *Times* because it is a respected, high-circulation, and influential newspaper of record in the United States. In terms of the substance of the article, I selected a piece on United States–North Korean relations that were a prominent issue in the news in mid 2019, which is important because individuals might be better equipped to identify nontruths compared to a less salient issue.

I then embedded the original and the synthetic stories into an online experiment, randomizing the treatments and asking whether respondents viewed the article as credible, whether they were likely to share the story, and if the story shifted attitudes about North Korea as a security threat. While most of the outputs were generally reasonable, I winnowed the outputs with minimal intervention, culling the noncredible stories and preserving the best ones, using three criteria to jettison the least credible stories: the presence of 1) grammatical or spelling errors (appropriate use of articles, complete sentences); 2) factual errors (correct titles/affiliations for named individuals); and 3) conceptual coherence (stays on topic vs deviates to unrelated topic).

---

[207] See Appendix for a complete discussion of the three experimental designs and instruments.

[208] "Better Language Models and their Implications," https://openai.com/blog/better-language-models/

One passage illustrates these potential output problems. Particularly in the less powerful model, some of the outputs were gibberish. In one egregious case, the synthetic story referenced Kimi Jong Un – later in the story corrected to Kim Jong Un – G-DNow News Staff, and then a long, frivolous paragraph about Easter:

> Life is a place full of surprises! Melt a glorious Easter cake in French but not that green. Well, a green cake, but for a Tuesday, of course! All Easter party year and here is the reason for baka.
>
> So here is the unsophisticated basket from my Emails with Moët: HOUSE – Magical Easter Treating for Outdoor Ahead, serving up latter too because the coconut would smell really good and it is about 32 °C/94 °F.
>
> Now lets make them during GF Parento Pinata – Yummy chocolate chip pancakes with dark chocolate frosting. Look how pretty you instincts are as they are meant for requirement. Topped with fresh pear, green chard, chive and Friday – peach drops and Play nice – marsh and date to finish.

Another story referred to Ted Lieu (D-Calif), chairman of the Congressional Foreign Trade Committee. Congressional committees are referred to as House or Senate, and no Foreign Trade Committee exists, let alone one on which he has a seat (he is on the House Foreign Affairs Committee). Moreover, states tend to be referred to by two letter abbreviations rather than as "Calif." Another story used the abbreviation DPRK and then followed with "DPRK is the initials of North Korean leader Kim Jong Un's father," which is inaccurate; it refers instead to the Democratic People's Republic of Korea. To test the concept of synthetic-text credibility, I filtered out stories with these types of errors and included the outputs with the fewest errors to locate a best-case scenario for the prospects of misinformation.

For the 345M parameter model, I selected three outputs based on a two-sentence input. What that means is that I fed the first two sentences from the original *New York Times* story into the text prediction tool. After running this initial experiment, and aiming to test the power of the model by feeding it a less wordy input, I used both two-sentence and one-sentence inputs for the two higher-power models (774M and 1.5B parameter models). For each category of model, I randomized the original *New York Times* story and the GPT-2–generated stories, running three separate experiments on Amazon Turk in July and August 2019. Given the theoretical interest in whether synthetic news can be confused for real news, I asked all respondents whether they viewed the story as credible or not credible (on a four-point scale), their likelihood of sharing the story on social media, and whether the story had shifted attitudes on whether they viewed North Korea favorably or unfavorably, and whether the threat posed by North Korea's development of nuclear weapons was a critical threat, important but not critical, or not important at all.[209]

Most important in terms of the theoretical question of whether synthetically generated news can pass for real news or instead whether it can be detected by readers is the question of credibility. Table 2 shows the results of the three different GPT-2 models.

In the 345M parameter model, respondents viewed all of the texts as more credible than not. Even in the treatment that respondents thought was least credible, three-fifths of people deemed the article to be credible, with the most credible story reaching almost 72 percent. Nonetheless, the differences between all of the treatments and the baseline *Times* story were large (the largest was about 25 percent) and all of those differences were statistically significant at well above the 0.05 level.[210] In short, human detection of the least powerful model was not terribly keen.

The 774M fared significantly better. Credibility of the one and two sentence inputs were virtually indistinguishable from the baseline *NYT* story. In the case of one of the one-sentence treatments, respondents expressed that the synthetic text was more credible (a mean of 84 percent) than the original *Times* baseline (71 percent), a statistically significant improvement over the original news article (above the 0.05-level). One reason may be that the first sentence of the *Times* piece leads as a focused topic sentence, whereas the second sentence proceeds to discuss the name of a North Korean ship, the *Wise Honest*, which is the real name but sounds fictitious and therefore provided seed material for a less credible-sounding GPT-2–generated story.

Next, I tested the most advanced model, the 1.5B parameter model. OpenAI had staged the release of its model and embargoed this particular model due to the concern for misuse. I conducted the experiment while the model was still unavailable to the public but available to researchers. However, this model fared no better than the 774M model. Although all treatments approximated the baseline, with no statistically significant differences between the treatments and the baseline, none had better credibility scores than the baseline the 774M model had been able to achieve.

The research design also allowed me to test differences between the treatments and the baseline condition in terms of whether individuals were likely to share the

---

[209] These questions are drawn directly from Gallup, https://news.gallup.com/poll/247151/far-fewer-americans-north-korea-greatest-enemy.aspx

[210] Zellers et al. similarly found comparable levels of trustworthiness (100 articles of news and propaganda) for a different natural-language model called Grover. Our findings further corroborate the plausibility of language models for manufacturing news stories. Rowan Zellers, Ari Holtzman, Hannah Rashkin et al., "Defending against Neural Fake News," https://arxiv.org/pdf/1905.12616.pdf

Table 2 Difference in means between three GPT-2 models and either 2 or 1 sentence inputs (relative to baseline *New York Times* article on the question of whether the news source is "credible"). *=p<0.05, **=p<0.01, ***=p<0.001

Treatment	345M			774M			1.5B		
	Mean (%)	95% CI	t	Mean	95% CI	t	Mean	95% CI	t
New York Times	83.4	77–99	–	71.0	61.9–80.0	–	76.1	67.9–84.4	–
2 sentence input (1)	58.3	49–67	4.5 ***	72.8	67.1–81.6	−0.29	74.5	66.9–83.9	0.12
2 sentence input (2)	71.7	63.7–79.8	2.24 **	65.4	56.1–74.7	0.86	71.0	61.9–80.4	0.84
2 sentence input (3)	68.75	61–77	2.78 ***						
1 sentence input (1)				83.8	76.5–91.1	−2.18 **	76.5	67.9–85.1	−0.06
1 sentence input (2)				75.2	66.7–83.8	−.67	70	60.8–79.1	0.99

social media story. I found that across all three experiments and all conditions, the likelihood that individuals would share the story did not vary at all relative to the baseline condition, with all of the conditions in the range of about 20–30 percent, though with no statistical differences among them. Synthetic news, in other words, did not appear to diffuse more prolifically than the real news.[211] To put those levels into perspective, a study of click-through rates – the percentage of people who click on a story or ad – for the targeted Facebook stories during the 2016 election reached as high as 13.4 percent, with most of the inflammatory posts around 4–5 percent, and a typical click-through rate for a Facebook ad or story reaching about 0.9 percent.[212] Although the null finding – that there were no differences between the likelihood that someone would share the synthetic text versus the original story – may seem surprising in its consistency, studies of viral content online show that divisive content is more likely to go viral, as is content that is high valence either positive or negative.[213] In the context of this finding, this study – which relied on discussion about the North Korea nuclear program either in *The New York Times* or a style emulating that newspaper – is unlikely to share those attributes of content that goes viral.

Lastly, I tested whether the stories were equally likely to change attitudes about North Korea. I looked at this possibility in a number of ways. One was to evaluate the within-subject change – probing the overall opinion of North Korea and attitudes about North Korea's nuclear program before and after the story – to see whether any particular story had an impact measured by either formulation of the question. None of the stories meaningfully changed attitudes within subjects. Nor were there any statistically significant differences across subjects. In other words, no particular story had a notable impact in either dampening or increasing the perception of threat compared to any other. Political persuasion is difficult, as many people have already made up their minds about many issues, and the evidence here is consistent with other studies that have found minimal impact of fake news on political behavior such as policy preferences.[214]

If the virtue of using this technology is that it allows for greater automation, then moving away from the human intervention employed in the previous study makes sense. The second experiment therefore more fully automated the

---

[211] Soroush Vosoughi, Deb Roy, and Sinan Aral, "The Spread of True and False News Online," *Science*, March 9, 2018, 359, No 6380, 1146–1151.

[212] DiResta et al., *New Knowledge* report, 37–38.

[213] Marco Guerini and Jacopo Staiano, "Deep Feelings: A Massive Cross-Lingual Study of the Relation between Emotions and Virality," *WWW 2015 Companion*, May 18–22, 2015.

[214] Guess et al, "Exposure to untrustworthy website in the 2016 US election."

approach of synthetic text generation. In this experiment, I used the same *New York Times* story as the baseline and randomized the one-sentence inputs from the three model sizes, with 200 stories per model (and therefore 200 respondents per model for a total of 600 respondents on Amazon Turk).

In addition, I sought to understand what individuals were thinking when they responded that a story was "credible." While individuals may have imputed different understandings to the word credibility, there is no reason to think that those understandings would have changed in systematic ways across the experiments, which means that variation in the perceptions of credibility could reasonably be attributable to differences in how believable the story seemed. Moreover, the use of "credible" to judge a story is consistent with the question wording of firms such as Pew, which use "credibility" as a proxy for the believability of a news outlet,[215] and Roper, which has long queried perceptions of credibility of different media outlets to assess the relative advantages of various news forms.[216]

Nonetheless, credibility, even if it approximates ideas of believability,[217] may mean different things to different people, but the initial experiment was unable to shed particular light on the features of the AI story that are persuasive to readers. Recognizing the potential multidimensionality of credibility, I engage previous scholarly work that has used credibility indexes that capture some combination of factual accuracy, trustworthiness, bias, and believability.[218] By way of comparability, I ask individuals whether they thought the story was credible. I then disaggregate the potential features of credibility by asking the degree to which the story was believable, accurate, and clear.[219] To create a credibility index, I asked respondents to code each of those factors – believability, accuracy, and clarity – on a one-to-four scale (very, somewhat, not very, and not at all) and then aggregated and plotted the credibility distribution of the

---

[215] www.people-press.org/2012/08/16/further-decline-in-credibility-ratings-for-most-news-organizations/

[216] Matthias Kohring and Jorg Matthew, "Trust in News Media: Development and Validation of a Multidimensional Scale," Communication Research, 34 (2007), 231–252.

[217] Philip Meyer, "Defining and Measuring Credibility of Newspapers: Developing an Index," Journalism Quarterly, (1988), 573.

[218] Andrew Flanagin and Miriam Metzger, "Perceptions of Internet Information Credibility," *Journal of Mass Communication Quarterly*, 77, 3 (Autumn 2000), 515–540; Thomas Johnson and Barbara Kaye, "Cruising Is Believing?" Comparing Internet and Traditional Sources on Media Credibility Measures," *Journal of Mass Communication Quarterly*, 75, 2 (Summer 1998), 325–340.

[219] I exclude depth or completeness because I select a fairly narrow foreign policy issue of North Korea within one type of media source, a hypothetical newspaper, whereas the depth or thoroughness measures are geared toward comparison of different media types, for example, newspapers, magazines, and candidate literature, which are qualitatively different in terms of their theoretical and actual depth measures (Johnson and Kaye, 2000, 328–329).

indexed score.[220] I also asked open-ended question about what individuals had in mind when they responded that the story was credible or not credible.

Results

Figure 5 plots the credibility distribution of the three models, with 200 individuals per model, and an aggregated index based on believability, accuracy, and clarity. As Figure 5 suggests, the two most powerful models converged with a relatively high credibility score compared to that of the least powerful model.

In open-ended replies, respondents who viewed the story as credible commented, for example, that "it had facts that can be trackable, information as to why something happened, and was written professionally." Another said, "it came off as an actual news story posted by/about the United Nations and about the United States involvement with the seized ship." More generally, the credulous respondents wrote about the "very trustworthy" or "pretty real and believable" nature of the story, or that "it seemed credible given the current state of affairs."

Those who were less convinced offered specifics to justify their attitude. One respondent said, "it did not read like a news article, and there were a couple of errors." Others said that there were "scant details, weird wording," that "the article was difficult to comprehend, which in my experience is unusual for an online article," that "it is not a news story that I would likely find in

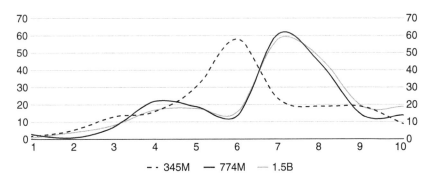

Figure 5 Credibility distribution (index of 1–10) for the 355M, 774M, and 1.5B GPT-2 model sizes. Y-axis is number of respondents (n=200 per model). Credibility index based on a four-point scale of whether the story was 1) believable, 2) accurate, and 3) clear, then aggregated to a 3–12 scale and rescaled to be between 1 and 10. The y-axis is the number of respondents out of the ~200 whose credibility index registered at that 1–10 level.

---

[220] Flanagin and Metzger, "Perceptions," 522.

a newspaper – the geopolitics don't seem right, and the tone is off," that "there may be some truth to the story, but don't believe there was extensive research," or that they had identified a "grammatical error early on." One respondent said, "there is a lot of fake news on the internet. I believe the story has about a 75 percent chance of being credible."

Other criticisms consistently concentrated on the lack of citations or credible sources, and in some cases flagrant factual errors: "If you read the story it makes no sense. It talks about the US and North Korea fighting two long and bitter nuclear wars." In the face of ambiguity or internal inconsistency,[221] evidence suggests that respondents were prone to confirmation bias both in terms of the style and substance of the content. In terms of substance, many respondents reported that the prospect "seemed realistic enough" given the ongoing tensions between the United States and North Korea. Beyond substance, individuals responded that the style of the story itself seemed realistic, corroborating their perception of how a "real" news story would appear: a United Nations location, Korean-sounding names of government officials, and historical context that was all plausible. The psychological dynamic suggests that motivation bias may inflate credibility scores, even if individuals cannot follow the precise content, while not necessarily changing their beliefs, a question we take up in the next experiment.

If analyses of online disinformation are any indication, malicious actors tend to spread divisive content on "hot-button issues with racial undertones," thereby stoking social discord in the United States. The previous experiments used a story on North Korea to understand and compare credibility measures, and while the topic of the story did engage an ongoing policy issue, it is not the type of socially divisive story that malicious actors would likely create or amplify.[222]

To understand the potential consequences of these more politically charged disinformation campaigns, I carried out a third study on immigration, which has policy salience and is divisive. In summer 2019, at the time of this study, Gallup measured immigration as the most important issue by the highest percentage of Americans ever recorded.[223] The topic focused on immigration caravans that were migrating from central America to the United States border. To understand how individuals respond to media that comports or conflicts with their ideological priors, I varied the ideological angle of the story.

[221] Vosoughi, Roy, and Aral, "The Spread of True and False News Online."

[222] Maggie Miller, "Senate Intel Report," *The Hill*, October 8, 2019.

[223] Jeffrey Jones, "New High in US Say Immigration Most Important Problem," *Gallup*, June 21, 2019, https://news.gallup.com/poll/259103/new-high-say-immigration-important-problem.aspx

As a baseline story, I selected a descriptive story about immigration caravans from the *Associated Press.* I then selected one story from *Fox News*, seen as a credible source for Republicans and distrusted by 81 percent of liberals, and another from *The Huffington Post*, known to have a progressive bent and viewed as credible by liberals and overwhelmingly distrusted by conservatives.[224] Scholars who have studied the effect of countervailing media exposure suggest that partisans are both able to identify the ideological orientation of media accounts and then also see bias in news stories that oppose their partisan priors. If this is the case, then conservative respondents would be able to identify the *Fox News* article as conservative and believe that it is a credible news source, and vice versa for liberals. Correspondingly, a story consistent with one's partisan priors would be more likely to animate or exercise individuals, and an opposing story would have little effect.[225]

The experimental design consisted of a 3x3 design. A total of 1,500 respondents were randomized and read original stories associated with the left, center, and right. A second parameter consisted of a one-sentence input for a GPT-2–generated story (using the most powerful model, the 1.5B parameter model). I then also varied the stated authenticity of the article, channeling the false flag warnings that social media outlets have issued on their sites to alert readers to potentially false or misleading stories.[226] At the top of the story, I crafted a banner with the following disclaimer, warning in red, bolded ink, among other things, that "this article contains false or misleading information, possibly intended to incite anger or strong emotion. Don't be fooled."

As in the previous experiments, I asked about the credibility of the story as well as about attitudes toward immigration, looking to understand whether the provocative, synthetically generated stories changed attitudes, including as a function of partisanship, whether the source bears ideological consistency, and whether the story is labeled with a media disclaimer. Borrowing from Gallup questions, I asked whether respondents favor or oppose the construction of walls along the US border.

Beyond assessing whether warnings or disclaimers are likely to work, I was interested in how the partisanship of both the story and the respondent interact to influence the perceived credibility of the story and attitudes about the issue in question, immigration. The research of Clayton et al. suggests that partisanship is likely to condition both the credibility of the headline, especially in the context of

---

[224] Amy Mitchell, Jeffrey Gottfried, Jocelyn Kiley, and Katerina Eva Matsa, "Political Polarization and Media Habits," *Pew Research*, October 21, 2014.

[225] Kevin Arceneaux, Martin Johnson, and Chad Murphy, "Polarized Political Communication, Oppositional Media Hostility, and Selective Exposure," Journal of Politics, 176.

[226] Katherine Clayton, et al. 2019. "Real Solutions for Fake News? Measuring the Effectiveness of General Warnings and Fact-Checking Tags in Reducing False Belief in False Stories on Social Media." *Political Behavior* https://doi.org/10.1007/s11109-019-09533-0.

Trump-approving individuals exposed to pro-Trump stories, or "rated false" story and Trump approval, with pro-Trump individuals less likely to believe anti-Trump headlines in general but especially with false tags. While these news stories were not about Trump, they aligned either with or against his positions on immigration (either pro or anti). Previous studies might therefore suggest that Republicans would view the *Fox News* stories as more credible than either the *Huffington Post* or the Democrats' views on the credibility of either right or left.

The main theoretical expectations of this third experiment hinged on how partisanship influences the perceived credibility of synthetic text, whether it affects participant responsiveness to disclaimers about synthetic news, and whether the disclaimer, even if it erodes the perceived credibility of the story, succeeds or fails to change views about immigration. To test these expectations empirically, I first compared the Republicans' view of the GPT-2–generated *Fox News* story with Democrats in terms of whether they think the story is credible, and conversely, whether Democrats were more likely to sympathize with the GPT-2–generated story based on the *Huffington Post*. The analysis suggests that individuals did view the stories through their partisan lens. Republicans generally thought all of the stories were somewhat credible, including the AI-generated stories. In terms of the disclaimer, however, the differences between the *Fox News*–based AI story with and without the disclaimer were not distinguishable, whereas Republicans were quicker to jettison the credibility of the *Huffington Post* AI-generated story once it had a disclaimer.

Democrats, in contrast, expressed less trust in the AI-generated story across outlets, but also showed a significant drop in credibility for the *Huffington Post* story compared to the *Fox News* story, where the credibility was low to begin with and the disclaimer had no additional marginal impact. The difference between Republicans and Democrats on this issue is consistent with Clayton et al., who find that Republicans are far more credulous of the pro-Trump story than Democrats of either the pro-Trump or anti-Trump story.[227]

Lastly, I assessed whether the disclaimer affected attitudes about immigration on the basis of partisanship. To do so, I looked at how Republicans and Democrats responded to the disclaimer versus nondisclaimer GPT-2 story for both the politically congenial story and the noncongenial story. On this question, I consider the effect on attitudes about building a wall between Mexico and the United States to see whether Republicans, for example, mute their antagonism to immigration when they read the *Fox News* story with a disclaimer versus the GPT-2–generated story without the disclaimer. Conversely, we investigate whether Democrats' enthusiasm for immigration declines when they see the

---

[227] Clayton, "Real Solutions for Fake News?"

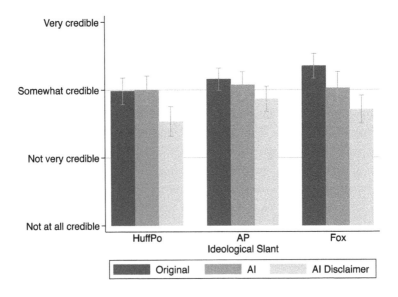

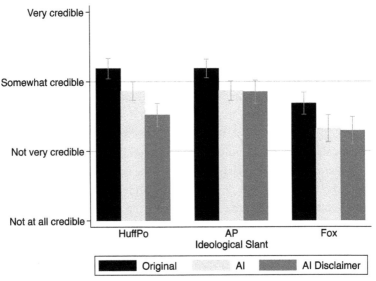

Figure 6 Credibility of news story among Republicans(top panel) and
Democrats(lower panel)

disclaimer, or whether both parties are sufficiently routed in their attitudes about
immigration that these disclaimers have no effect.

As Figure 7 suggests, the stories themselves had almost no effect on attitudes.
Republicans support building a wall irrespective of the credibility of the story.
They may not see the disclaimer stories as credible but their attitudes after
reading the story are not affected by that information of potentially fake or

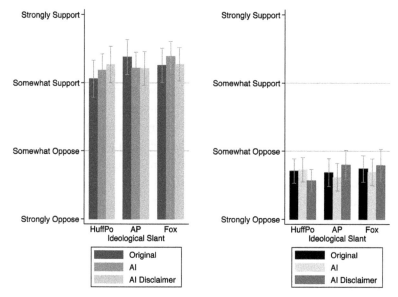

Figure 7 Attitudes toward wall by party identification (Republicans left panel, Democrats right panel)

fabricated news. The same is true for Democrats, who decidedly oppose building a wall irrespective of the news they read.

Given existing studies on the effect of media and disclaimers on public attitudes – many of which coalesce around the "minimal effects" thesis that suggests that media effects are both limited and fleeting – the prospect of persuasion is fairly dim. Broockman and Green, for example, found that online advertising by political candidates recalled exposure to advertisements but that exposure did not translate into changes in the candidates they supported.[228] The reason is that individuals have strong analytical or philosophical priors, and the media environment is noisy, so exposure often has negligible effects.[229] On the other hand, some scholars have found that under some conditions – arguments in opposition to a policy initiative or messages that vary in intensity[230] – media messages can indeed shape attitudes.

By extension, the prospect for disclaimers to impact attitudes faces limits. Confirmation bias is a powerful force, such that people find credible the

---

[228] David Broockman and Donald Green, "Do Online Advertisements Increase Political Candidates' Name Recognition or Favorability? Evidence from Randomized Field Experiments," *Political Behavior*, 36, 2 (2014), 263–289.

[229] William McGuire, "The Myth of Massive Media Impacts."

[230] Michael Cobb and James Kuklinski, "Changing Minds: Political Arguments and Political Persuasion," *American Journal of Political Science*, 41, 1 (Jan 1997), 88–121; 90; John Zaller, "The Myth of Massive Media Impact Revived: New Support for a Discredited Idea," in *Political Persuasion and Attitude Change*.

perspectives that accord with their preexisting notions, and are reluctant to disavow themselves of previously held beliefs. Clayton et al.[231] have found that certain types of disclaimers and warnings employed by Facebook do reduce the perceived accuracy of stories – both the false and true stories – but neither disputed nor rated false tags reduced individuals' willingness to like or share the fake news stories, meaning that they do nothing to reduce the viral nature of the story. Other studies suggest, however, that warnings can attenuate the degree to which people believe false claims, reduce the consumption of misinformation, or counter confirmation bias when it comes to embracing scientific claims.[232]

Taken together, the results suggest that citizens often view GPT-2–generated text as credible in similar ways that they view actual news stories, and in some cases more credible than an actual news story. These attitudes, though, are heavily conditioned on partisanship. Republicans tend to be fairly credulous of news stories in general, but quick to be dismissive of a left-wing story with a disclaimer. Democrats tend not to believe the stories on the right – original, synthetic, or disclaimer – even though they are never told that these stories come from *Fox News*. The content evidently speaks for itself in terms of partisan leanings and does not come across as credible to Democrats regardless of the form it takes. In some senses, the stickiness of attitudes about immigration in the face of fake news is encouraging. Republicans tend to oppose more immigration and support a wall, Democrats support more immigration and oppose a wall, irrespective of the story or its disclaimer, suggesting that immigration may not necessarily be an issue where fake news can change attitudes much. Correspondingly, the results suggest that there may be other issues where synthetic news could be more effective in shifting attitudes, perhaps those where attitudes are less entrenched. Gun control or gun control, if this analysis is right, would be less susceptible to inflammatory fake news than newer issues where public attitudes are somewhat more inchoate.

Discussion and Conclusion

If the prospect of AI-generated news proliferates, given the ease and affordability, then the information environment will be increasingly clogged with news whose veracity is hard to judge. Indeed, this analysis shows that the more powerful the text prediction model, the more credible individuals find it, especially beyond the lowest capacity model. Credulity may lead either to

---

[231] Clayton et al., "Real Solutions for Fake News."

[232] Ullrich Ecker, Ziggy O'Reilly, Jesse Reid, and Ee Pin Chang, "The Effectiveness of Short-Format Refutational Fact-Checks," British Journal of Psychology, March 2, 2019; Toby Bolsen and James Druckman, "Counteracting the Politicization of Science," Journal of Communication, 2015.

complete confusion or incredulity of anything, which most likely means simply cueing off their political partisan elites.

The question is what can a democratic society do as an antidote to the mass production of fake news, the news that individuals will seek out to inform them on foreign policy? One possibility, given that these AI-generated stories some-times produce erroneous facts, is for Americans to double down on fact check-ing. A large majority of Americans (79 percent) report that they fact check news stories. That said, they may be less inclined to do so when the article seems credible than when it is apparently fake.[233] Moreover, the high levels of cred-ibility of at least two of the fabricated news stories calls into question previous surveys showing that 59 percent of Americans had seen fake news, or those surveys indicating that 84 percent of individuals are very or somewhat confident that they can recognize fabricated news.[234] It may be that individuals actually cannot perceive meaningful differences, or that at the least, these manufactured stories are credible enough to pass as real news. Thus, the broader issue may be the cognitive confusion that has resulted from the contemporary media envir-onment, in which individuals cannot necessarily discern differences and that they are left either overly credulous or unwilling to believe anything. In a 2016 poll, Pew found that 88 percent of Americans believed that made-up news had left them confused about basic facts.[235] Confusion about basic facts, however, means an opening for malicious actors who would seek to exploit ambiguity and division.

While perhaps disconcerting from the standpoint of democratic governance, the analysis offers some glimmers of hope. Even though individuals reported that all of the AI-generated stories were fairly credible, they often hinted at features of the story that they found other than convincing. On the one hand, the evidence points to confirmation bias, in which individuals were seeing the trappings of a real news story – references to goings-on at the UN for example, official-sounding names and titles, etc. – as confirmation of authenticity. On the other hand, comments suggesting that the story did not sound right open the door to potential digital-literacy interventions. Such interventions might consist of public service announcements about the features of fake news, for example, data on the proliferation of fake news, perhaps thereby encouraging individuals to trust their judgments and skepticism when they see details that look incorrect.

---

[233] David Graham, "Some Real News about Fake News," *The Atlantic*, June 7, 2019.

[234] Darrell West, "Brookings Survey Finds 57% Say They Have Seen Fake News during 2018 Elections," *Brookings*, October 23, 2018.

[235] Amy Mitchell, Jesse Holcolm, and Michael Barthel, "Many Americans Believe Fake News is Sowing Confusion," *Pew Research*, December 15, 2016.

Beyond these prospects for human detection, other potential avenues of countermeasures include technology itself. Since AI technology is "familiar" with the algorithms that went into the text prediction, it might also be able to detect AI-generated outputs. AI-generating tools such as a program called Grover have achieved detection rates of about 73 percent, far better than the 25 percent human detection rates observed in this study, suggesting that a machine might be the antidote to a machine. But only certain "machines." One online hack purported to detect neural network–written text, except that it was rife with errors. The false positives were high – for example, it identified an excerpt from James Joyce's *Ulysses* as almost certainly fake text ("a 0.04 percent chance of being real"), same with text from a President Trump speech.[236] The tool is clever, but also makes clear that the measure–countermeasure is a cat-and-mouse game; a small improvement or change to GPT-2 would render this tool ineffective.

Until now, Russia has been able to amplify news by employing people in the Internet Research Agency who find, create, and amplify divisive or ideological news, but their efforts have reached a ceiling because of limits to manpower. New tools such as GPT-2, however, create what *The Verge* refers to as

> an automated trolling machine, spitting out endless bile and hatred. If it becomes more sophisticated and able to persuade and convince in a reliable fashion, it could cause even subtler damage, influencing debate online. Countries like Russia and Saudi Arabia, which already employ thousands of online propagandists to abuse government opponents and push official talking points, could scale up their efforts overnight. And remember, none of the text GPT-2 produces is copied and pasted: it's all newly generated, thus harder to filter and more easily shaped to specific ends.[237]

If the threat can be both created and deployed so easily, why has it not necessarily been done? One reason may simply be that until now, the technology has been inadequate. Beta versions were plagued by grammatical, factual, or spelling errors. More recent, more powerful versions are more credible and less error prone. That GPT-2 has not become a trolling machine may simply mean that the technology was not ready: now it is, and the malicious actors can now roll out credible bile and hatred.

Another possibility has to do with the connection between information and power. The more frequently a tool is used, the less powerful it becomes. Would-be malicious actors would want to deploy the information strategically to maximize the impact. If the Internet Research Agency planned to use this

---

[236] https://twitter.com/JanelleCShane/status/1196567777697382400
[237] James Vincent, "OpenAI's New Multitalented AI Writes, Translates, and Slanders," *The Verge*, February 14, 2019.

type of tool, for example, it may not want to exhaust its impact well prior to an important election but wait and deploy it closer to the time of the election to maximize the impact. Deep fakes offer a valuable comparison. When fake videos of Nancy Pelosi or Mark Zuckerberg were unveiled, they at least initially seemed convincing. Now the public's defenses are primed so the "nth" deep fake has less impact since people are less credulous. The technology has to be used sparingly since once it is used, someone is on the alert to catch it again.

Having identified the susceptibility of democratic audiences to social media influence, and the potential for malicious actors to exploit the insidiousness of social media in the democratic process of information acquisition, Section 6 turns to potential policy solutions. The public has shown that it is not at all adept at discerning differences between real and fake. Are democracies then at a permanent disadvantage in an era of social media or can regulatory changes remedy these vulnerabilities, and if so by whom and at what cost? The final section investigates those questions.

6 Digital Sovereignty

In November 2018, French President Emmanuel Macron and Facebook founder Mark Zuckerberg met in Paris. They announced a plan to collaborate on the removal of harmful content from the social media platform. While the partnership did not produce binding regulation, one French official referred to the partnership as an "unprecedented experiment" that would allow French authorities to understand Facebook's algorithms. As Macron explained, "We are giving blind faith to our daily digital tools. Today, when I see our democracy, internet is much better used by the extremes ... or by terrorist groups."[238] The partnership intended to cultivate ideas about how to regulate hate speech on the social network site. It also took a very different tack from the warnings of Senator Dianne Feinstein (D-CA), who told lawyers at Facebook, Google, and Twitter, "You created these platforms ... and now they're being misused. And you have to be the ones who do something about it – or we will."[239]

Feinstein suggested a substitutable role between corporate self-regulation and government regulation, although the Facebook hearings of 2018 revealed that neither government nor industry alone was perfectly equipped to navigate the line between free speech and maliciousness. Indeed, how to thread that needle remains one of the nettlesome and elusive questions about the role of social networks in international policies. Feinstein's threat that if social media

---

[238] Mark Scott and Zachary Young, "France and Facebook Announce Partnership against Online Hate Speech," *Politico*, December 11, 2018.

[239] Casey Newton, "Senators Blast Tech Companies over Russian Meddling: 'Do Something about It – Or We Will." *The Verge*, November 1, 2017.

platforms did not regulate content, the federal government would, raises the question of agency – in particular, whose responsibility it is to minimize the potentially negative political externalities that were made **manifest in the 2016 election and beyond**.

Another question is why, once the political consequences were increasingly apparent, Facebook still did not act more aggressively. Indeed, as a *New York Times* study of Facebook's guidelines found, "The Facebook guidelines do not look like a handbook for regulating global politics."[240] Instead, the self-regulatory standards for monitoring and removing nefarious content are vague yet extensive, intolerant yet inconsistent. The consequence, as the study noted, is that the rules "make the company a far more powerful arbiter of global speech than has been publicly recognized or acknowledged by the company itself."[241]

Governments around the world, however, have begun to assert themselves when it comes to regulating social media. The concluding section addresses the question of why social media companies did not operate aggressively, either proactively or retroactively, to address the way actors were able to use these platforms for nefarious aims. The generous answer is that the problem of regulation poses a number of murky freedom-of-speech issues and curtaining speech goes against the whole open ethos of the Internet. A less charitable interpretation is that social media firms have few incentives to moderate content, since doing so is both costly but also at odds with a business model that favors sensational content that attracts and keeps users online.

Into the relative regulatory void, states have begun to find their voice. Where once Twitter was seen as enormously disruptive to the Westphalian system, we are now seeing a resuscitation of a Westphalian state-based system, one where individual governments assert their digital sovereignty and push back against the amorphousness of data. They do so because technology firms showed that they are not substitutable with governments. Navigating the gray zone of free speech is not to their comparative advantage, nor is voluntarily giving up their entire business model that relies on data collection and individual curation of the news. Even still, the ability of governments to regulate social media, while not futile, is an unenviable task. Social media continues to shape-shift, evolving into new platforms with new hosts in different countries that present new national security considerations. It is a situation in which governments identify ways to foil threats or protect data, only to be faced with a new twist as the adversary innovates and ups its game.

---

[240] Max Fisher, "Inside Facebook's Secret Rulebook for Global Political Speech," December 17, 2018. www.nytimes.com/2018/12/27/world/facebook-moderators.html
[241] Ibid.

Why Companies Do Not Regulate Like Governments

Feinstein's warning that if social media did not regulate itself, the government would, suggests a substitutable role between corporate self-regulation and government regulation, although the Facebook hearings of 2018 revealed that neither government nor industry alone was perfectly equipped to navigate the line between free speech and maliciousness. Indeed, how to thread that needle remains one of the nettlesome and elusive questions about the role of social networks in international policies. Feinstein's threat that if social media platforms did not regulate content, the federal government would, raises the question of agency – in particular, why these platforms have not minimized negative externalities that were made manifest in the 2016 election and beyond. At least initially, the reason why these platforms failed to act more like governments appeared to be a combination of corporate ignorance and technological determinism. Zuckerberg's initial approach betrayed a naïveté in terms of ethical questions about social networks: "move fast and break things" with an eye toward "domination" of social media, by which he meant a monopoly obtained by growing the numbers through network effects as quickly as possible.[242]

Consistent with that goal, Zuckerberg's main hiring target consisted of "just this group of computer scientists who were trying to quickly prototype and see what was possible."[243] Engineers had a software problem they were determined to solve: linking individuals together via an Internet platform. Because of its origins as a social networking site, it did it not necessarily anticipate the implications of being a news editor, structuring and filtering news in ways that would set the political agenda. By all accounts, the idea of an "algorithmically driven news feed" was not part of its initial ambition, even if the company acknowledges it has ultimately become a gatekeeper of news,[244] which had policy consequences that outpaced either self or government regulation.[245]

That Facebook and other social media firms were naïve in terms of their role in structuring the news and navigating the lines between free and hate speech or legal free speech and illegal foreign interference is not entirely surprising. Many of the lines between free speech and either hate speech or the incitement of violence are contested rather than reducible to either algorithms or a set of bullet points. Scholars have long debated the complexities of how to permit and promote freedom of speech, a cornerstone of democracy, while being sensitive to the way these rights might infringe on minority groups, for example. The debate centers on the line where positive rights (e.g., one's freedom of speech)

---

[242] Osnos, "Can Mark Zuckerberg Fix Facebook?"
[243] Franklin Foer, "Facebook's War on Free Will," September 19, 2017.
[244] Devito, "From Editors to Algorithms," 754.   [245] Foer, "Facebook's War on Free Will."

cross the line into negative rights, which requires that others not be harmed and that one abstain from an adverse effect on others.[246] Philosophical and constitutional questions about the lines of free speech form the basis of several Supreme Court cases in every term.[247] The cases often revolve around similar questions as those online, which is where one group's right to free speech becomes disparaging to another group. In a recent case, a band had sought to appropriate and register a derogatory term, which the Patent and Trade Office ruled unacceptable because it disparaged minority groups. The Court ruled in favor of the band, with Justice Alito concluding that "[permitting] the suppression of any speech that may lead to political or social 'volatility,' free speech would be endangered."[248]

That the case made it to the Supreme Court is an important reminder that these free speech disputes are typically settled by the courts, which are well-suited to adjudicating the ambiguous, nondeterministic lines related to the First Amendment. In contrast, the comparative advantage of an entity such as Facebook is not the type of political nuance necessary to mediate between legitimate and illegitimate groups on the political spectrum, or legitimate versus illegitimate angles on ongoing conflict. The platform has banned particular groups it deems to promote violence, such as the Proud Boys, a group of self-described "western chauvinists" that admits only men and claims to be anti–social justice without being alt-right. The Federal Bureau of Investigation declared that the Proud Boys are not an extremist group,[249] but the group and its founding member were banned for what Facebook deemed to be the promotion of violence in political protests. A Facebook spokesperson said, "Our team continues to study trends in organized hate and hate speech and works with partners to better understand hate organizations as they evolve. We ban these organizations and individuals from our platforms and also remove all praise and support when we become aware of it."[250]

The discrepancy between official governmental positions on speech and those of Facebook reveal the tensions in terms of mediating the gray area of political content. If political rights questions are difficult to adjudicate in a domestic context, they are more nettlesome where the context is foreign. The community standards that proscribe violence offer overarching guideposts

---

[246] Robert Nozick, *Anarchy, State, and Utopia* (Blackwell, 1975).

[247] www.freedomforuminstitute.org/first-amendment-center/supreme-court-cases/

[248] Matt Ford, "The Supreme Court Offers a Warning on Free Speech," *The Atlantic*, June 19, 2017.

[249] Keith McMillan and Eli Rosenberg, "The FBI Says the Proud Boys Are Not an Extremist Group after All," *The Washington Post*, December 7, 2018.

[250] Nick Statt, "Facebook Bans Accounts Affiliated with Far-Right Group the Proud Boys and Founder Gavin McInnes," *The Verge*, October 30, 2018.

but are limited when it comes to specifics, often leading to a set of ad hoc regulations.

Facebook moderators have allowed individuals to praise the Taliban but only in the context of the Taliban's willingness to enter into a cease-fire.[251] While the gesture toward political context is commendable, sentiment analysis is notoriously complicated in general, and parsing an individual's or group's "willingness" for a cease-fire would be no easy task. Lacking political context altogether, a Facebook manual that blacklisted terrorist groups included the Free Syrian Army (FSA), which has engaged in guerrilla-style activities but is both an ally of the United States and an opponent of the Bashar Al-Assad regime, which has engaged in chemical weapons attacks against its people. The United States does not consider the group to be involved in terrorist activity, and Russia, which aligns with the Assad regime, has corroborated that the FSA is not a terrorist group and rather is part of any political solution to the conflict in Syria,[252] yet moderators were instructed to remove FSA content.[253]

The Balkans, with a history of antipathies, illustrates the types of challenges these platforms face. Pages revealed to *The New York Times* showed presentations and spreadsheets with titles such as "Western Balkans Hate Orgs and Figures" that seeks to navigate the lines between mainstream and fringe groups. Facebook planned, for example, the Knights Templar International group, a group that takes hardline views on Muslim integration, and acts as a "living shield and sword for the defense of Christian communities."[254] The guidelines also include errors that make manifest the political information deficit that the company faces. Ratko Mladic, who was a Bosnian Serb General during the Yugoslav wars, was listed as a fugitive war hero despite having been captured, put on trial, and found guilty of war crimes in the International Criminal Tribunal for the former Yugoslavia.

In Pakistan, of 64 organizations banned by the government for extremist ideologies, 41 remain on Facebook, accounting for more than 700 pages and groups, excluding the individual user profiles themselves. As the newspaper *Dawn* concluded based on an in-depth investigation, the perpetuation of extremist sites is "disturbing evidence of the confusion that prevails in the state apparatus about what constitutes the real threat" to the country, a criticism against the government for pursuing "red herrings and its muddled

---

[251] Max Fisher, "Inside Facebook's Secret Rulebook for Global Political Speech."

[252] Michele Nichols, "Russia Says US-backed Free Syrian Army Not a Terrorist Group," *Reuters,* October 1, 2015.

[253] Nick Hopkins, "Facebook Struggles with 'Mission Impossible' to Stop Online Extremism," *The Guardian,* May 24, 2017.

[254] Lawrence Marzouk, "Facebook Pulls Pages Linked to Rightists Active in Balkans," *Balkan Insight,* October 4, 2018.

priorities."[255] Flipped on its head, however, the observation could also be an indictment of Facebook's decision rule, and whether, as Zuckerberg acknowledges, executives "sitting in an office here in California" are the appropriate people for determining how to make decisions that best reflect the democratic process across the world.[256] As the investigation acknowledged, some of the groups the government bans are not associated with the promotion of violence, but do "advocate the overthrow of the democratic system," which raises questions about the basis of Facebook's ban. The decision rule is all the more important because Pakistan has an official media blackout on Election Day, but Facebook *is* permitted, which makes it a focal point for debates and developments on the day of voting, granting an advantage to groups that are permitted by Facebook but proscribed by the government.

A second impediment to self-regulation is that these entities are ultimately businesses focused on generating revenue and maximizing profit. Because the services are free, however, the firms collect vast amounts of data about users in ways tantamount to monitoring their behavior with either no consent or non-explicitly granted consent. Having collected data about how users buy products online, for example, platforms have information valuable to third-parties that can hyper-target users through advertising. Critics refer to the business model as "surveillance capitalism," which Shoshana Zuboff says "unilaterally claims human experience as free raw material for translation into behavioral data."[257]

The line of critique has led to a series of congressional testimonies that seek to understand social media's use of consumer data. In one of the initial hearings, Chairman of the Senate Commerce, Science, and Transportation Committee John Thune (R-SD) justified the scrutiny by saying, "Our joint hearing will be a public conversation with the CEO of this powerful and influential company [Facebook] about his vision for addressing problems that have generated significant concern about Facebook's role in our democracy, bad actors using the platform, and user privacy."[258] Facebook is the most visible, public social media face but the concerns raised through Facebook are endemic to social media more broadly, where regulation has lagged.

Regulation has always lagged behind disruptive technology. The printing press and the steam engine had enormous political and economic effects that eventually produced laws and regulations related to property rights and contract

---

[255] "Banned Groups on Facebook," *Dawn*, May 31, 2017.

[256] Quoted in www.vox.com/the-big-idea/2018/4/9/17214752/zuckerberg-facebook-power-regulation-data-privacy-control-political-theory-data-breach-king

[257] Shoshana Zuboff, *The Age of Surveillance Capitalism: The Fight for a Human Future at the New Frontier of Power* (Public Affairs, 2019), 8.

[258] "Facebook, Social Media Privacy, and the Use and Abuse of Data," www.commerce.senate.gov/2018/4/facebook-social-media-privacy-and-the-use-and-abuse-of-data

law.[259] Regulatory lags are almost inevitable because policy risks are unknown, the opportunity cost of legislators' time is high – creating incentives for a wait-and-see approach[260] – and few legislators have the technological background to understand the nature of the regulatory challenge, and in a way that does not trample on freedom-of-speech democratic foundations.[261]

Self-regulation, however, has also lagged because it is at odds with the business model, which is based on traffic and online engagement. Anger, as discussed earlier, can drive engagement as much a virtue signaling. Social media platforms, as companies that increase revenue through traffic, have incentives to allow viral, and by association often-divisive content, on their platforms. Facebook defends the action as free speech, "making the world more open and connected." As one observer put it, "Like many other major tech platforms the company doesn't seem capable of openly reckoning with or articulating what it means to be a powerful political actor in a major conflict – and this might have something to do with the fact that the only real consequences they face are bad PR and not loss of market share or legal liability."[262] To be sure, Facebook is simply capitalizing on human emotion, but the conflicts of interest brought about by the need to generate revenue are brought into sharp belief by the contrasting case of its Chinese counterpart. The Chinese microblogging site, Weibo, has stringent censorship and limits content distribution, meaning it limits both the original content and its potential viral effect. Communist party officials embed themselves in the social media platform to ensure that Weibo heeds party orders, suggesting that corporate will has considerable bearing on how sites weigh and act on the trade-offs between moderation and open distribution.[263]

Facebook found itself embroiled in a public relations crisis after the election, fallout that saw the company lose $37 billion in market value in just one day.[264] The company began to see convergence between social responsibility and its corporate welfare, but even conditional on recognizing a need for self-regulation,

---

[259] Vivek Wadhwa, "Laws and Ethics Can't Keep Pace with Technology," *MIT Technology Review*, April 15, 2014.

[260] David Mayhew, *Congress: The Electoral Connection* (Yale University Press, 1974).

[261] Larry Downes, "How More Regulation for US Tech Could Backfire," *Harvard Business Review*, February 9, 2018.

[262] Ingrid Burrington, "Could Facebook Be Tried for Human-Rights Abuses?" *The Atlantic*, December 20, 2017.

[263] Gary King, Jennifer Pan, and Margaret Roberts, "How Censorship in China Allows Government Criticism but Silences Collective Expression," *The American Political Science Review*, 107, 2 (2013): 326; Jeffrey Shen and R. Miles McCain, "Deciphering Chinese Censorship," https://papers.ssrn.com/sol3/papers.cfm?abstract_id=3266193, October 2018.

[264] Chris Isidore, "Facebook's Value Plunges $37 Billion on Data Controversy," *CNN*, March 20, 2018.

the challenges are steep. Because of the enormous volume of data, with about 1.62 billion people logging on to Facebook every day and producing content,[265] Facebook relies heavily on artificial intelligence (AI) to spot violent content. Its AI tools, trained by human moderators, identify 99.5% of terrorist-related posts that are removed, 98.55% of fake accounts, and 86% of graphic violence posts. However, AI detects only 38% of hate speech–related posts that are ultimately removed, pointing to imperfections in its AI tools. One reason is that sentiment analysis is inherently imperfect. Individuals might use "jihad" either literally or figuratively, for example. Another reason is that since the AI tools are trained by human moderators, and the moderators have been far scarcer in other languages, Facebook's AI is not nearly effective in languages other than English.[266] The difficulty across languages is particularly pronounced for languages that do not use the Roman alphabet. Burmese script, for example, has a peculiar font that posed challenges for computer screens, "making it difficult to identify racial slurs or other hate speech" according to Facebook.[267] Zuckerberg acknowledged that AI would need about five to ten years to "recognize the nuances."[268]

Human moderators are an obvious complement to AI but are far more expensive and have therefore been relatively scarce because they cut into declining operating margins. As of April 2018, Facebook had 7,500 moderators judging whether symbols match a terrorist group's or whether language violates hate speech guidelines.[269] Chief Operating Officer Sheryl Sandberg testified in 2019 that Facebook also employs 30,000 people to regulate the platform for misinformation or hate speech, a five-fold increase over 2017. She acknowledged that early efforts had been insufficient in preventing actors from trying to "sow disinformation and dissent into societies."[270]

The Myanmar case illustrates the challenges of self-regulation. Moderating the anti-Rohingya vitriol would have run counter to the user experience by filtering out the types of content with which individuals engage most – the anger-inducing material – and therefore challenging operating margins. To be

---

[265] "The Top 20 Valuable Facebook Statistics – Updated October 2019," https://zephoria.com/top-15-valuable-facebook-statistics/

[266] Jason Koebler and Joseph Cox, "The Impossible Job: Inside Facebook's Struggle to Moderate Two Billion People," *Motherboard*, August 23, 2018.

[267] Steve Stecklow, "Why Facebook Is Losing the War on Hate Speech in Myanmar," *Reuters*, August 15, 2018.

[268] www.washingtonpost.com/technology/2018/08/16/facebook-turns-artificial-intelligence-fight-hate-misinformation-myanmar/?utm_term=.c420ac5cfbd2)

[269] Julia Carrie Wong and Olivia Solon, "Facebook Releases Content Moderation Guidelines – Rules Long Kept Secret," *The Guardian*, April 24, 2018.

[270] Mike Butcher, "Stung by Criticism, Facebook's Sandberg Outlines New Plans to Tackle Misinformation," *Tech Crunch*, January 20, 2019.

most successful in challenging the military's incitement of violence, the company would also have had to hire attorneys, local-language speakers, and likely a local office, all of which would further erode margins.[271] The United Nations admonished the company for entering the Myanmar market without understanding a country with volatile ethnic and religious tensions, and urged better area knowledge as a precursor for launching country-specific versions of its platform.[272]

Facebook ultimately responded by conducting a study in which it spoke with sixty individuals in Myanmar, a so-called "human rights impact assessment" that appears to have culminated in a program codenamed Project Honey Badger, a monitoring program it outsources to Accenture based in a Kuala Lumpur office, which handles monitoring in a number of Asian countries. The firm hired its first two Burmese speakers in 2015, with about sixty people reviewing reports of hate speech and other content posted by Myanmar's Facebook users. By comparison, to match the user-to-moderator ratio in Germany, Facebook would have had to hire 700 moderators in Burma.[273] Facebook itself hired three full-time Burmese speakers at its international headquarters in Dublin, arguing that outsourced content monitoring is more efficient because the companies with which it partners are specialists in such operations. Outsourcing also meant that, as Facebook confessed, "it was impossible to know to be definitive on that [how many Burmese speakers the company had hired.]"[274]

While the 2016 election eroded Facebook's credibility in ways that began to redress the conflict of interests in terms of more aggressive monitoring, the approach is inherently reactive. Platforms cannot commit human monitors to every country, and inevitably will triage the problem: it commits monitors to countries such as Germany where the government tends to exercise an active agenda in reining in privacy violations – which has a deterrent effect given the cost of violations[275] – and Russia and Iran, known to have large numbers of cyber troops engaged in misinformation. It is more inattentive to a range of countries that either seem to pose little threat of misinformation and or have governments that do not threaten Facebook with regulatory fines, such as Austria. In the middle, cases such as Myanmar that did not seem to warrant

---

[271] Antonio Garcia Martinez, "Why Facebook's Thinning Profit Margins Are a Secret Asset," *Wired*, August 6, 2018.

[272] Casey Newton, "One Easy Thing Facebook Should Do in Myanmar," *The Verge*, November 10, 2018.

[273] Anthony Kuhn, "Activists in Myanmar Say Facebook Needs to Do More to Quell Hate Speech," *NPR*, June 14, 2018.

[274] Stecklow, "Why Facebook Is Losing the War on Hate Speech in Myanmar."

[275] Butcher, "Stung by Criticism."

monitors, will flare up and prompt self-regulatory responses that are both dilatory and inadequate.[276]

Responding to legislative and international pressure for accountability, and a growing sense of "techlash" – public pushback against technology firms – Zuckerberg also floated the idea of a "Supreme Court" of Facebook. The proposed independent tribunal would seek to advance a "more democratic or community-oriented process" for community standards about free speech, promote transparency and accountability about the decision rule for acceptable speech, and develop an independent appeal process. In May 2020, Facebook announced that it would follow through on the idea, establishing a Supreme Court for speech and appointing nine law professors, a Nobel Peace Prize laureate, journalists, and free speech advocates to issue rulings about content moderation.[277]

As this section suggests, social media firms' incentives to regulate, and tools for doing so are problematic – finding the appropriate balance between permissiveness and proscription – which has left something of a regulatory void that national-level governments are increasingly stepping in to fill. These too are imperfect and evolving as the technology evolves and unintended consequences of particular policy solutions are made manifest.

Digital Sovereignty as Neo-Westphalianism

That social media, which provides news that can inform, but also distort or entrench individuals' policy choices, poses threats especially to democratic governance is increasingly apparent. That the completely unmitigated flow of that information, without any degree of monitoring or control, would present problems – an enormous proliferation of child porn and hate speech beyond the pale – is also fairly uncontroversial. What that regulation should look like, however, is highly controversial. It is not surprising that those answers are not rooted in international but national-level answers that reflect national-level norms, laws, and values.

Just as the twenty-first century seemed to usher in a degree of data commoditization, made most manifest in the 2016 American election, the equal and opposite reaction appears to be in the direction of digital sovereignty. Digital sovereignty, the idea that internet users can decide how their data is used and distributed,[278] has asserted itself as a way to push back against the concerns about the commoditization of data in the twenty-first century. With the growing recognition that free speech considerations are subjective and culturally

---

[276] Max Fisher, "Inside Facebook's Secret Rulebook," *The New York Times*, December 27, 2018.

[277] David Ingram, "Facebook names 20 people to its 'Supreme Court' for content moderation," NBC, 6 May 2020.

[278] Jaqueline Bargmann, "What Do We Know about Digital Sovereignty?" www.polyas.de/blog/en/digital-democracy/digital-sovereignty, June 13, 2016.

contingent, and that the incentives of social media companies are at odds with taking assertive stances in regulating content, countries themselves have increasingly stepped in to reassert their primacy over the transnational flow of data. The scope of sovereignty can be at the level of the individual who controls data about himself by using encrypted communication or opting out altogether, or at the supranational level, with the European Union taking measures with which member states must comply, but are increasingly a national-level decision that reflects national-level values about privacy and free speech.

States have resuscitated themselves in part because of regime-type differences. Autocracies are, in many respects, more vulnerable to the organizing consequences of social media, which can allow protests to overcome collective action in ways that might be threatening to a regime. They also have mechanisms of control that are compatible with an autocratic regime type. Democracies, by contrast, have limits to the degree to which they can control individual access to the Internet, which makes them more vulnerable to foreign or malicious actors even while their populace is free. Democracies themselves, however, manifest differences for several reasons.

One is that the United States tends to have more antipathy toward government regulation than Europe, for example. In the United States, therefore, the default appears to be sabre-rattling by Congress and Big Tech responding with the suggestion that individuals rather than the government or tech firms self-regulate. The differences are overdetermined, however, because the companies to be regulated are not outside actors, as American Big Tech is in Europe, but American companies that have triggered fewer sovereignty concerns because they are inherently more accountable to the American government and because the US government is less concerned about the nexus between data and national security than it would be with a foreign company.

In Europe, the attention to privacy manifested in part through the General Data Protection Regulation, requiring technical and organizational measures to protect individual privacy, including at the individual member state level. German Chancellor Angela Merkel has asserted that the European Union would assert "digital sovereignty" to manage and store its own data, the purpose being to reduce dependence on US-based storage services offered by Amazon, Microsoft, and Google. She followed up by saying that these companies collect vast amounts of data that they can train to understand consumer habits in ways that create "dependencies." Germany has launched a cloud initiative called Gaia-X for European data storage. The hope is to alleviate the increasing reliance on German companies such as Volkswagen that store their data on Microsoft and Amazon servers, undermining their sovereignty. Merkel has tried to accelerate solutions to the growing reliance on both American and Asian data storage, warning that "there is a great danger that we end up being too slow, that while we are still debating the philosophical question of data sovereignty, the world just rolls over us."[279]

In China, the government has asserted its own form of digital sovereignty through the Great Firewall, which prohibits access to many social media sites and censors that craft pro-regime messages while limiting access to those that undermine the regime. Myanmar, which had come under international scrutiny for the military's use of Facebook to incite violence against the ethnic minority group, the Rohingya, has responded with its own form of digital sovereignty in two ways. One is that it reached out to Facebook for country-specific guidance on governance. Facebook faced criticism because of its dearth of Burmese-speaking content moderators, only two in 2015 at the height of posts that had provoked violence.[280] Monitoring, in other words, is language and country specific, which is another way in which digital sovereignty manifests itself. Second, in the wake of negative publicity, the Myanmar government, and in particular the military, has issued defamation complaints against those who criticized it for inciting violence and hoarding the country's wealth. Those defamation suits, which further illustrate the reassertion of digital boundaries, are adjudicated by Myanmar courts.[281] The government's overall approach embraces the idea that a country-specific offense is the best defense against international and domestic criticism.

Countries such as China and Russia have attracted attention for their emphasis on "internet sovereignty" but the fact is, almost every country has governed the internet in ways that are consistent with their own domestic laws and with an eye toward upholding "national honor and interests." While the Internet was founded on openness and sharing the same protocols, countries have found and are finding new ways to control access and amplification of news online. In other words, as one technology journalist put it, "the world wide web has fractured into a series of state-wide webs, each controlled in distinctive ways."[282] In short, while the Internet may have started as an open, connected, post-Westphalian construct, the nation-state has pushed back and reasserted authority.

---

[279] Guy Chazan, "Angela Merkel Urges EU to Seize Control of Data from US Tech Titans," *Financial Times*, November 12, 2019.

[280] Olivia Solon, "Facebook's Failure in Myanmar Is the Work of a Blundering Toddler," *The Guardian*, August 16, 2018.

[281] Richard Paddock and Saw Nang, "Myanmar Military Uses Threat of Prison to Stifle Criticism ahead of Elections," *The New York Times*, August 17, 2019.

[282] Samuel Woodhams, "The Rise of Internet Sovereignty and the End of the World Wide Web?" *The Globe Post*, April 23, 2019.

Looking Ahead

The social media world is a world of flux. Facebook, dominant in the social media world for more than a decade, is now slipping from its perch. Political controversies such as those involving the 2016 American election or the Myanmar genocide have prompted conversations about Facebook's business model and the way it collects and monetizes user data. Advertisers have become wary of Facebook's public image and brand safety.[283] *Washington Post* journalists observe that most of their Facebook traffic has plummeted as the platform's credibility has waned.[284] Younger demographics are flocking to platforms like Instagram and Snapchat as alternatives, with Russian trolls following on their heels. A report on the 2016 election found that Russian disinformation campaigns posted on Instagram 116,000 times in the first six months after Trump's election, twice the number of posts of Facebook.

In tandem, the countries that use social media strategically have proliferated. In 2017, only thirty-five countries had political disinformation campaigns. By 2019, the number of countries where at least one political party was engaging in social media manipulation – for example, using hacked or stolen social media accounts to silence dissent, as in Guatemala – had doubled to seventy.[285] The tactic is relatively inexpensive, does not require much tech know-how, is generally plausibly deniable, meaning that it is difficult to link definitively with a government source, and is unlikely to prompt aggressive retaliatory measures by the target.

Russia has garnered the most media attention because of the 2016 election, but allegations suggest that China is moving into the interference business. President Trump used his speech at the United Nations General Assembly meeting in September 2018 to say, "We have found that China has been attempting to interfere in our upcoming 2018 election … against my administration." Although he was not specific, the charges are plausible. China vowed in 2006 that it would "strengthen the construction of foreign-related media and networks that promote China," and to "innovate in foreign propaganda methods."[286]

The Covid-19 pandemic highlights China's efforts to spread divisive and conspiratorial content in a foreign audience. Long focused on targeting its own domestic audience with pro-regime content, leaving the foreign propaganda campaigns to Russia, China used the pandemic to practice new approaches.

[283] Erica Perry, "Report: Facebook and Google Are Losing Ad Dominance," *Social Media Week*, March 21, 2018.

[284] Thanks to Henry Farrell of the *Washington Post*'s Monkey Cage politics blog for bringing this to my attention on January 28, 2019.

[285] Alba and Satariano, "At Least 70 Countries Have Had Disinformation Campaigns."

[286] Rush Doshi and Robert Williams, "Is China Interfering in American Politics?" *Lawfare*, Oct 1, 2018.

Those include misinformation campaigns more closely associated with Russia that seek to undermine trust in government institutions. In the context of Covid-19, examples include emphasizing the American death toll, the shortage of personal protection equipment, or the American origins of the virus. The Chinese Foreign Ministry spokesman, Zhao Lijian, would frequently take to Twitter to promote any of these narratives in an unapologetically bombastic manner. In one tweet, Zhao posted a video of the Center for Disease Control director saying CDC was caught on the spot. When did patient zero begin in US? How many people are infected? What are the names of the hospitals? It might be US army who brought the epidemic to Wuhan. Be transparent! Make public your data! US owe us an explanation![287]

Tensions about the origins and handling of the pandemic have mixed with underlying, pre-existing tensions on trade and technology to create simmering distrust that some observers suggest could verge on a new Cold War.[288] Against this backdrop, the United States government has looked with increasing scrutiny at China's acquisitions of popular American social media companies. One of the most visible examples is the US Treasury Department's investigation of a social media platform called TikTok, a Chinese social media platform that hosts short videos that are often musical or comedic. While TikTok does not operate in China, it is enormously popular in the United States and in 2018 passed Facebook, YouTube, and Instagram to become the most downloaded application.

Against this backdrop, the United States government has looked with increasing scrutiny at China's acquisitions of popular American social media companies.

One of the most visible examples is the US Treasury Department's investigation of a social media platform called TikTok, a Chinese social media platform that hosts short videos that are often musical or comedic. While TikTok does not operate in China, it is enormously popular in the United States and in 2018 passed Facebook, YouTube, and Instagram to become the most downloaded application. The national security concern stems from the collection of vast amounts of data, which is the basis of TikTok's artificial intelligence algorithms that allows the platform to offer personalized content to users. A bipartisan group of US senators has expressed concerns on two fronts. One is that Chinese censors engage in censorship, often blocking content that is unfavorable to the Chinese government such as the Hong Kong protests or videos related to the Xinjiang camps that house Uigur minorities. Perhaps more importantly,

---

[287] https://twitter.com/zlj517/status/1238111898828066823?lang=cs

[288] Chris Buckley and Steven Lee Myers, "From 'Respect' to 'Sick and Twisted': How Coronavirus Hit US-China Ties," *New York Times*, 17 May 2020.

however, the TikTok parent firm maintains a close relationship with the Communist government. One of the most valuable commodities for the government is access to demographic data, which the AI models need to generate predictions about individual behavior. TikTok's assertions that "we have no higher priority than earning the trust of users and regulators in the US" or that the US user data is not "subject to Chinese law" have done little to allay US investigatory concerns.[289]

Relatedly, new challenges arise as nondemocratic countries such as China take ownership of popular social media platforms such as TikTok. In December 2019, TikTok suspended the account of an Afghan-American woman who had posted a video that was ostensibly about eyelash curling, but where in the same breath she denounced the Chinese treatment of minority Uighurs in China. The video went viral and the company asserted that the video had violated community standards, but the episode raised important questions about the intersection between regime type, social media content and consumption, and international politics.[290]

Democratic targets such as the United States also appear to be learning how to adopt countermeasures against their vulnerability. Investigating the national security concerns of the way foreign governments might use social media is just one example. In the 2018 midterm elections, US Cyber Command reportedly disrupted Internet access of Russia's IRA, blocking their efforts at election interference to a point at which IRA employees complained to system administrators, which suggests a degree of disruption that had impact while not necessarily raising immediate flags about the source. The counterfactual level of election interference is unknowable, but even if the disruption had temporary impact, officials who anonymously commented on the report rightfully acknowledged that "causing consternation or throwing sand in the gears may raise the cost of engaging in nefarious activities, but it is not going to cause a nation state to just drop their election interference or their malign influence in general."[291] In addition, the distribution of viral content takes place far upstream of the election, in which case disrupting access during the election is a very partial measure, not to mention the countermeasures that Russia takes to block disruption in the future.

These examples suggest that social media continues to evolve, but irrespective of the form and function it takes, many of the pillars on which social media

[289] Richard Altieri and Benjamin Della Rocca, "US Launches National Security Probe into Chinese-Owned App TikTok," *Lawfare*, November 8, 2019.

[290] Lydia Emmanouilidou, "Tiktok Apologizes to US Teen after Removing Video Critical of Chinese Government," *PRI*, November 29, 2019.

[291] "US Cyber Command Operation Disrupted Internet Access of Russia's Internet Research Agency," *Washington Post*, February 26, 2019.

influence rests will remain fairly constant. Thus, while legislative attention and many of the examples in this Element have focused on Facebook as a platform for covert, asymmetric, information and psychological warfare, the implications go well beyond. Technology companies, founded by engineers determined to solve and refine a software problem – linking individuals across time and space – will continue to have political consequences whether that company is Facebook or other analogous platform in the future, such as Reddit, YouTube, or TikTok. Offense is likely to have an advantage because the Internet is open-access, technology firms are likely to be reactive rather than proactive about the regulatory challenges that might address the adverse political consequences of the platform, and the algorithms are likely to remain susceptible to manipulation even if technology companies mount their best efforts at disrupting inauthentic users and removing disinformation. Social media platforms are engaged in a game of cat and mouse, in which it can change policies and adjust algorithms, but ill-intentioned actors can simply adapt and find a slightly different tack of manipulation.[292]

New applications that are based in China present a different set of questions for democratic use of social media than when the platform was a US-based company such as Facebook. What is the new nexus of national security and social media? In what ways might foreign, nonallied actors use the troves of data to generate machine-learning algorithms that create strategic disadvantages or asymmetries? Are there ways to restore trust in media institutions that has eroded from a proliferation of fake news, including AI-generated fake news? These are evolving and therefore unanswered questions but ones that will likely all be answered against the backdrop of a surging sense of digital sovereignty, in which individuals, national governments, and regional institutions assert their voice and provide their own value-specific antidotes to the seemingly amorphous creep of the Internet and data that characterized the early years – in other words, just a decade ago – of social media.

---

[292] Adam Satariano, "Europe Worries as Facebook Fights Manipulation Worldwide," *The New York Times*, August 22, 2018.

Cambridge Elements $\equiv$

International Relations

Series Editors

Jon C. W. Pevehouse
University of Wisconsin-Madison

Jon C. W. Pevehouse is the Vilas Distinguished Achievement Professor of Political Science at the University of Wisconsin-Madison. He has published numerous books and articles in IR in the fields of international political economy, international organizations, foreign policy analysis, and political methodology. He is a former editor of the leading IR field journal, *International Organization*.

Tanja A. Börzel
Freie Universität Berlin

Tanja A. Börzel is the Professor of political science and holds the Chair for European Integration at the Otto-Suhr-Institute for Political Science, Freie Universität Berlin. She holds a PhD from the European University Institute, Florence, Italy. She is coordinator of the Research College "The Transformative Power of Europe," as well as the FP7-Collaborative Project "Maximizing the Enlargement Capacity of the European Union" and the H2020 Collaborative Project "The EU and Eastern Partnership Countries: An Inside-Out Analysis and Strategic Assessment." She directs the Jean Monnet Center of Excellence "Europe and its Citizens."

Edward D. Mansfield
University of Pennsylvania

Edward D. Mansfield is the Hum Rosen Professor of Political Science, University of Pennsylvania. He has published well over 100 books and articles in the area of international political economy, international security, and international organizations. He is Director of the Christopher H. Browne Center for International Politics at the University of Pennsylvania and former program co-chair of the American Political Science Association.

Associate Editors

Jeffrey T. Checkel *Simon Fraser University*
Miles Kahler *American University*
Sarah Kreps *Cornell University*
Anna Leander *Graduate Institute Geneva, Institute of International Relations (PUC-Rio), and Copenhagen Business School*
Stefanie Walter *University of Zurich*

About the Series

Cambridge Elements in International Relations publishes original research on key topics in the field. The series includes manuscripts addressing international security, international political economy, international organizations, and international relations theory. Our objective is to publish cutting edge research that engages crucial topics in each of these issue areas, especially multi-method research that may yield longer studies than leading journals in the field will accommodate.

Cambridge Elements ≡

International Relations

Elements in the Series

Lightning Source UK Ltd.
Milton Keynes UK
UKHW022322060820
367837UK00007B/42